© Jeremy Kelly

REGGIE HOUSER HAS THE POWER
is Helen's fifth novel. She lives just outside
Sheffield and has worked as an actress for
many years. She now prefers writing the
stories rather than starring in them and
can be found tapping away in her writing
room with her Whippet, Billy, for company.

@HelenRutterUK
www.helenrutter.com

Also by Helen Rutter

The Boy Who Made Everyone Laugh
The Funniest Boy in the World
The Boy Whose Wishes Came True
The Piano at the Station

REGGIE HOUSER HAS THE POWER

Helen Rutter

SCHOLASTIC

Published in the UK by Scholastic, 2024
1 London Bridge, London, SE1 9BG
Scholastic Ireland, 89E Lagan Road,
Dublin Industrial Estate, Glasnevin, Dublin, D11 HP5F

Text © Helen Rutter, 2024
Illustrations © Andrew Bannecker, 2024

The right of Helen Rutter and Andrew Bannecker to be identified
as the author and illustrator of this work has been asserted by
them under the Copyright, Designs and Patents Act 1988.

ISBN 978 0702 31465 0

A CIP catalogue record for this book
is available from the British Library.

Printed and bound in Great Britain by Clays Ltd, Elcograf S.p.A
Paper made from wood grown in sustainable forests
and other controlled sources.

FSC
www.fsc.org

MIX
Paper | Supporting
responsible forestry
FSC® C018072

1 3 5 7 9 10 8 6 4 2

www.scholastic.co.uk

CHAPTER ONE

SUMMER FAIR!!!

Pocket money is in the green sock. Don't spend it all on the chocolate fountain like you did last year — you vomited in the parents' shelter, remember?

"Put your bottom on the seat, Reggie, please."

The second the bell rings, I jump up. I do every day. The bell has rung. School's over. That's what the bell means, isn't it? Once my bum has left the chair it's almost impossible to put it down again. Even though Mrs Wheatley is waiting with high eyebrows and pursed lips, I can't actually force it to make contact with the chair, however hard I try. My brain knows

1

it's time to go so my body is going, as though it's being controlled by the bell.

I squat as low as I can and wrap my arms around the desk, as if I'm hugging it. Anchoring myself as close to the chair as I can. Jiggling my hands and feet underneath while the droning voices of thirty kids sound out, "Good afternoon, Mrs Wheatley. Good afternoon, everybody."

I've never heard kids sound so miserable as when they say the end-of-the-day good afternoons. I always try to be the loudest and make it sound more fun. But then I get looks, as though it's not meant to be fun.

"Your adults will be waiting on the field. Enjoy the summer fair, everyone, and I will see you tomorrow for our very last day together."

I'm up. My bum can leave its seat. I run. For once it's not just me. We all run. Henry and Roman get through the door first, followed by the rest of the popular kids. Hilly and Reena and Tilly all giggle and skip outside together. All the kids who have loved every second of primary school, and all the ones who, like me, have not. We all rush to the door. The kids who have found their best friends at primary school and have sleepovers every weekend and the ones who have arguments and change friends every other week. For once all of us want the same thing, to get out of this classroom as quickly as we can.

Today is one of those rare days where what's going on outside matches what's going on inside my brain. Noise, colour, voices and music all overlapping. Everything asking for attention at the same time. You would think that would be a good thing, but as soon as I hear the noise of the air going into the bouncy castle and see the crowd of chattering parents, my brain starts "zoning out". That's what Mum calls it when there is too much going on and I freeze. Sometimes it's in noisy, busy places like this or sometimes it's just when there's too much to do, and I don't know where to start.

Like this morning, when Mrs Wheatley had put my "to-do list" on the board.

I have a board at home and a board at school where I can put things I want to remember. At home I have these cool little magnets and colourful cards and I write down ideas and draw pictures of things that I don't want to forget. Mostly just silly stuff like trying not to vomit in the parents' shelter, but sometimes it's really useful. It's a bit like I'm talking to myself. They are all overlapping and fighting for attention like an explosion of colourful thoughts. Mum says it's like looking at my brain on a wall.

At school Mrs Wheatley writes the list. There are no colourful cards or cool magnets; it's just a boring list of the same old stuff I have to do every day.

I was doing number one – "Put your coat on the peg" – and I dropped my water bottle and water went all over the floor, but the list didn't mention dropping a water bottle. I kept looking at the board, which was telling me to put my coat on the peg, so I put my bag next to the water and carried on to the peg but then Kitty Turner tripped over my bag and landed in the water and I turned and looked at the board, looked at my coat and then looked at Kitty lying next to my bag and my water bottle… and it's all too much. Kitty Turner's sad face was not on the list. How was I meant to know what to do?!

When Isla went over to help her up, she scowled at me and whispered loud enough for me to hear, "At least we won't have to see his annoying face all summer." That made it even harder to know what to do. I could hear her voice for the rest of the morning, overlapping in my head with the sound of other voices and memories of all the horrible things the popular gang have said to me. When I've annoyed them they always have the same look on their face, like I'm not really human but something strange and disgusting. It makes me want to change every single thing about myself.

I watch them all at break, the way they talk and laugh, the way they lean on the wall, how they move. When any of them tell me how annoying I am, I try my hardest to be more like them. To stop fidgeting and shouting out answers, to flop into a chair instead of sitting up tight. To stop my brain from whirring, and change myself from the inside. It only ever works for five minutes, then I'm back to being annoying and disgusting again. It doesn't feel very good being me.

At the fair I manage to cut through the noise and find Mum and the Squealers. The Squealers are the kids that Mum childminds. They are called Una, Bea and Mabel, and they're all three. I find them by the Hook-a-Duck, squealing as usual.

I head down the hill behind the cake stall, finally feeling free from the faces and the noises of the classroom. I relax and let my feet go. Running and then rolling. Leaving the mayhem at the top, the volume changing on the way down, my thoughts rolling around my brain. When the hill runs out, I lie there and let everything settle, enjoying that today, for once, no one is standing over me and scowling, or angrily telling me to get up. For some reason, today I'm allowed to roll. School fairs and goodbyes mean rolling is OK. How am I meant to know that? Apparently leaving maths or science to run and roll is not so cool.

This may be the very last time I roll down this hill. I must have made myself dizzy on this school field hundreds of times. Before I started rolling I used to just run down it, let my body go, so that my head felt like it was going to outrun my feet. The rolling was a happy accident when one day it did. I wonder if there is a hill at my new school, although eleven is probably too old to roll. I will need to try my hardest not to be weird at Redbrook to have any hope of making friends. Mum says it's a whole new start and there will be loads of kids like me there. I'm trying not to get too excited in case it doesn't happen, but I can't stop imagining what it might be like to actually find some mates. A group of kids that don't hate me and don't look at me like I am a weirdo. Maybe I can find someone who secretly likes rolling too.

It was in Year Three when we found out why my brain is different from other people's. I did tests and quizzes and talked to a man with hair growing out of his ears. He asked me how I was doing at school and what I found difficult and then gave me a biscuit. Afterwards Mum sat me down with a fake bright smile and sad eyes and told me I had ADHD.

"That's why you are so busy, Reg."

I get called all sorts of things. Busy, buzzy, bubbly, fizzy, whizzy. I sound like a drink or a sherbet sweet. Sometimes I *feel* like a sherbet sweet. That makes it sound a bit more fun than it actually feels though. I don't think my brain would be as sweet as sherbet; it would probably taste a bit more like a lemon – a bit much. I wish I knew what it was like to have someone else's brain so I knew the difference. I've always wanted to be like everyone else but maybe everyone else's brain is like a boring old loaf of bread. There is no way of me ever knowing and that makes me feel a bit weird and sad.

My brain gets really busy when I want to say something, or tell a story, or answer a question and my mum or the teacher won't let me. Then I get really fizzy, like a Mento in a bottle of coke that's not allowed to pop. Then I get super wriggly and jiggly and try not to climb on the table but can't help it. Just let me answer the question! I know the answer!

7

I know it! I have to say it! I just have to! If I know the answer or really need to tell you something why not just let me?

"The other children need thinking time, Reggie."

"Keep it in your head, Reggie."

"Tell me at break time, Reggie."

"Write it down, Reggie."

"Whisper it to a teddy, Reggie."

"Not now, Reggie."

POP!

Miss Olsen was the best. She was my teacher in Year Three. When I was having a very "busy day" she would let me do five minutes of work and then go and run down the hill and back. That's when I discovered rolling and never grew out of it. She also gave me a teddy that I could whisper my answers to so I could let them all out and give the other kids a chance to speak too. I swapped the teddy for a plastic Spider-Man that fits in my pocket after Roman and Henry started throwing the teddy around at lunch and calling me a baby. I don't think I will take Spider-Man to Redbrook. I don't want anyone to see me whispering to a plastic superhero; that would not be a good start.

Miss Olsen was the one who knew that my brain

was different. She was the reason we went to see the man with the hairy ears. Not much changed after we found out. He said I could take tablets to slow down my brain but Mum hates medicine. She didn't even take paracetamol when she nearly cut the end of her finger off when she was chopping a carrot. So she said, "No, thank you," took the leaflets he offered, went home and ordered about a billion books on ADHD. Nothing she tries ever really does much good though, and she is so fed up of me getting in trouble and rushing around that I keep expecting her to bring out the tablets and shove them in my gob.

As the dizziness fades and I zone back in, I realize this is it, the end of primary school. One more day tomorrow and then it's all over. I'm so happy to get out of this hot classroom forever. I'm trying not to think about the classrooms and corridors of Redbrook. I have six whole weeks before I have to worry about secondary school but sometimes thoughts pop in before I can stop them. Excited ones that tell me it's going to be great, that I will make friends and have the best time ever. They are nice thoughts but they are always followed by louder ones that make me feel scared. It's a much bigger school so will there be even more kids who don't like me?

DO TRY THIS AT HOME!

THE PENDULUM

Find some string, an old shoelace,
or steal some wool from a granny's
knitting project. Tie a key or ring or
something small but heavy (no, not
your baby brother or your pet guinea
pig) to the end, so that it hangs freely
and evenly at the end of the string.
Hold it in the air and ask a question.
If the pendulum swings clockwise, it
means yes and anticlockwise means
no. (Be patient — sometimes it takes
a while for it to make up its mind.)
If you ask your mum for more pocket
money and the pendulum says yes, it's
pretty much a legally binding contract.

CHAPTER TWO

RED 240–260

Raffle tickets are in the envelope in the junk drawer. Do not forget to take them! They were a rip off and Mum said that Mr Pillbert is such a tightwad he probably wouldn't let me have the shoddy prize if I won but had forgotten the tickets.

A loudspeaker at the top of the hill announces the raffle. I stagger back up in time to hear Mr Pillbert the head teacher say, "The winner of the grand prize, a two-night all-inclusive stay at Trontin's holiday park is…" He picks out a ticket and opens it and I'm sure I can see him roll his eyes a tiny bit as he reads the name and number. "Red 241. Reggie Houser."

"Mum! Mum! We won! Mum!" I shout, holding my ticket in the air. "Mum!" I keep shouting until I see her. "Mum! Mum! Mum! Mum! We won! Mum!"

"Yes, I heard, Reggie." Her face has gone red as though she's embarrassed. I'm not sure why winning a prize could make you feel embarrassed though.

"I'll go and get it!" I say, thinking it will help.

"No, Reggie—" But before she can finish, I'm gone. I dash up to the stage and grab the envelope from Mr Pillbert's sweaty hand.

I squeak, "Cheers, Big Ears!" at him and all the kids laugh so I stick my tongue out, do a curtsey and then run straight back to Mum, throwing the envelope up in the air for her to catch.

"Let's go home, Reggie." She sighs, as if I've done something wrong again, even though I can't think what that would be.

I pretty much always feel like I've done something wrong. Even when I haven't a clue what it is. It makes me feel like a bad person. I can tell from the faces. Teachers lower their heads and do a long blink, Mum sighs and rubs her eyes, kids whisper and stare. Then I can either try and figure out what it is that I've done or just carry on and pretend I haven't seen the faces.

It's not a great feeling to be annoying. When my brother Kai lived with us, I used to annoy him on purpose sometimes. Repeating everything he said in a high-pitched voice or sticking notes on his back. That felt totally different. Being annoying then was funny, but when I'm not meaning to it's not funny at all. It makes me feel like I'm a terrible person.

Kai moved out a month ago. I cried when he left and he called me a softie, but in a way that made me feel embarrassed. I don't think I have ever seen Kai cry. He moved in with four of his mates and they play Xbox all night, drink beer and play tricks on each other. He looks so happy, and they have so much fun, it makes me want to grow up straight away and live with my friends. Although I don't really have any friends.

Some kids find it funny when I get into trouble, like Evan and Breeze. They aren't in the popular gang and so I think maybe they will hang out with me. They laugh when I'm messing about and tell me to keep going, so I do, even if it gets me into trouble. It feels good making them laugh. It feels like we're mates, but then they don't let me join in at break times when they are sitting and swapping cards. They always say I ruin everything.

Then there is Frizz, but she doesn't count because she's not at my school. She's my mum's friend Jane's daughter so she has no choice but to hang out with me when they come over, and anyway she's a girl. I want a group of mates that I can play Xbox all night with or prank, like Kai has. I want to playfight and wrestle like Roman and Henry do, with all the other popular lads cheering them on. I want a gang.

On the way home I'm doing three quick steps and one slow one and the Squealers are all copying me. Mum starts rubbing her eyes.

"What's up, Mum?"

"Nothing, sweetie, the summer holidays just feel like a long time, that's all."

"A long time with me, you mean? What did I do?" I stop the walking thing and try and walk in time with her. Mum has been sighing more than ever recently; I know it's my fault but I just don't know why.

"'Cheers, Big Ears' to Mr Pillbert? You are completely covered in mud and grass stains. We were at the fair for all of ten minutes. I've had three calls about your behaviour this week, Reggie. I'm exhausted."

"Oh," I say. I thought it had been a good day. I guess I was wrong.

"You really need to find a way to control that mind of yours, Reg."

"But I don't know how, Mum," I say sadly. I feel like I'm always going to disappoint her and make her rub her eyes.

Since Kai left it's been just me and Mum. Dad works away for six weeks at a time. He lays pipe for big building projects and has to go and stay wherever the job is. He calls all the men he works with by their second names or has nicknames for them, like Tink or Ruddy. They seem more like a family to him than we are sometimes. They are like his gang. I don't understand why Kai and Dad have found a gang so easily when I am finding it so hard.

When Dad comes home, he's big and loud in the house and he never sits down on the sofa. I once heard him and Mum arguing outside the back door and she said it was easier when he was away. That really confused me because she said it when he was in the middle of trying to fix the shed door, which is a helpful thing to do, surely?

I don't think it's easier when he's away. I thinks it's lonelier and sadder, and I want him to get another job and be home all the time. Even if he paces around, looking for things to fix, and never sits on the sofa. He says he likes his job and that we need the money, but I would rather never buy anything again and have him at home all the time.

Dad always has "projects", like fixing things and building things. Once he built a whole new car out of bits of old cars. It didn't start but it looked really cool. It's still down by the shed. Mum calls it a rust bucket and a waste of time. It wasn't a waste of time though. He let me help and it was so much fun. Sometimes he starts a new project before he has finished the one he is doing and then Mum gets really annoyed. I understand that though; sometimes you just get bored and want to move on. Me and Dad are pretty similar I think. That's why I miss him so much.

"How many days until Dad's back?" I ask.

"A couple of weeks, Reg."

"At least we've got a holiday to look forward to, Mum. We won!"

"I'm not sure I can manage it, Reg. Just me and you in a holiday park. I don't think so. Anyway, I've got the girls."

"But we won. Please, Mum. Please! We haven't

been on holiday for ages. You said the other day you needed a break."

"That's not quite what I meant, Reg."

"But we are not doing anything this summer, Mum. You can read one of those books you like, and there is a pool. I will take my bike and just ride and swim all day. There will be loads of kids I can hang out with so I can leave you to relax. I won't get into trouble, I promise."

I can see that she is wobbling so I try and look extra cute and carry on.

"We have to. You know we won't get a holiday otherwise. Dad is working and Kai won't go away with us. I will be too old soon so let's do it while we can and it's free! You haven't got the girls next week, have you? They're on holiday. It's perfect. Please, Mum. Pleeeeeeese!"

"How about this. Pleeeeeeeeeese can you get through your last day without causing any trouble?"

"Yeah!"

"No phone calls home. No running out of the classroom or coming back covered in mud. No forgetting your coat or your bag or your shoes! No drawing all over your hands with Sharpie or falling off your chair." As she is listing all of the things I can't do, I wonder if I will be able to do it.

"Just one day where you find a way to stay out of trouble?"

"Then we can go to Trontin's?"

"Then we can talk about it."

"I'll try, Mum. I promise." A huge grin is taking over my face. I skip ahead and jump out at the Squealers, making them scream louder than ever.

Surely I can be a normal boring kid for once. It's just for one day, after all.

DO TRY THIS AT HOME!

ROCK, PAPER, SCISSORS

The next time you play this game ask your opponent a question just before you start. They will answer and then most likely choose scissors, so pick rock and destroy them. Mwah ha ha ha!

CHAPTER THREE

VERY IMPORTANT!!!

My cue lines for the school play:

"Mrs Wheatley thinks we are all angels, of course."

"We will never turn into grumpy teenagers."

"How did a flamingo get into the classroom?"

DO NOT FORGET OR THE WHOLE CLASS WILL SCOWL AT YOU AGAIN.

Everyone is wearing their leavers' hoodie. Everyone apart from me. I lost mine the second day I had it. I chose yellow and had "Reggie Roo Roo" put on the back. When I came home in just a T-shirt, Mum didn't shout at me like I thought she would. She just sighed and said, "Of course you've lost it, Reg."

It feels weird today. The head teacher's goodbye assembly makes Hilly and Reena cry, and I even see Mrs Wheatley wipe her eyes. We're all going to the same secondary school so I'm not sure why it feels so strange and big. We'll see each other in six weeks.

Mrs Wheatley decided to put me in charge of the music for the leavers' play. The whole school come and watch and everyone makes a big deal out of it and counts their lines and gets stressed about costumes.

At first I was in the play but I kept changing my lines and said something different every time. Apparently, the people after me never knew when to speak so I was put on music instead. I quite liked being on stage; it felt like everyone was in a team, practising lines and all getting nervous together. Mrs Wheatley said the music is a really important job too but I don't feel like I am part of the team any more. I kind of wish I hadn't kept changing the lines, even though they were much funnier my way. When Mrs Fredricks, the office lady, came into a rehearsal I made her laugh so hard that she snotted.

I'm sitting at the side of the hall with my headphones on, in front of the computer, idly playing with the mouse. I click between the music screen, which has a list of all the songs in order, and an app called Fart World. The other day when the rehearsal got so boring I put both headphones over my ears and listened to farts for half an hour, before Mrs Wheatley shouted at me for snorting too loudly. I had to do something to entertain myself, watching the play over and over again and not being in it was the most boring thing in the world.

Mrs Wheatley told me that I'm only allowed to listen to the show music now and I have to keep one ear open to listen for my cues and get the music in the right place. I have to line up the track with my earphones and then pull out the lead and press play at the right moment so that it plays over the big new speakers in the hall. It's pretty easy. The first track is the sound of violins and birdsong.

I look along the rows of kids as Mrs Wheatley is talking about how everyone was involved in writing the play and how proud she is. I drift off and start jiggling. The girls are all squeezed together, arms linked in their matching purple hoodies. The boys are giggling or whispering in their groups. I wish I wasn't on the side with the boring music. I should be in the play too. Then maybe someone would be linking my arm or whispering in my ear.

Everyone seems to have a gang. Dad with his workmates, and Kai in his flat. The Squealers all running around screaming together. Everyone except me. I would love to giggle and whisper or link arms or have a nickname, but I always end up on my own. On the edge of everything. Watching it from a distance. I wish there was a way to find my own gang. People who think I'm great. People who definitely don't find me annoying, or sigh and roll their eyes at me. As I'm sitting and wondering about how I might find my gang at Redbrook, how I might make people like me, I hear my name.

"Reggie!"

I look over to see the rest of the class up on the stage, all staring at me with angry faces, waiting for the music to play. Isla and her gang narrow their eyes from the silent stage and whisper.

"Of course he ruined it."

"He literally can't do anything right."

Mrs Wheatley says my name again and I panic, pull the headphone wire out and hit the space bar.

FAAAAAAART

PPPPRRRRRRRRPPPHHHHHHH

PFFFFFFFSHHHHHHH

A series of fart sounds play out loudly across the hall. The audience howls with laughter and Mrs Wheatley goes bright red and marches over to where I'm sitting. I look at her with panic and instead of stopping the farting, I freeze. Glued to my chair. Listening to the laughter but seeing the anger on her face, thinking about what Mum said yesterday, my brain unable to figure out how to make it better.

"I didn't mean—" I start to say, but she hits the space bar, pauses the farts and gestures to the performers to carry on.

"Are you going to tell my mum?" I whisper as she squeezes me off my chair and takes over the controls. She shushes me and points to the floor where she wants me to sit. Worries start busying up my brain.

What if they tell Mum that I ruined the last day of term and she won't take me to Trontin's?

Why do things like this only seem to happen to me?

Why does everyone else have friends and matching jumpers and I'm always looking in from the outside?

Then I look out at the lines of kids and as I catch some of their eyes they twinkle as they hold in their laughter. A kid from Year Two puts his thumbs up and nods at me. They think I did it on purpose. I keep looking. The Reception kids are still shaking with laughter. Maybe it's not so bad. It's only farts, after all, and they are funny. I raise my thumbs to the Reception kids and they wave at me, tears still rolling down their faces. I giggle too and stick my tongue out, rolling my eyes around in their sockets, making them laugh even more.

"Reggie!" hisses Mrs Wheatley's voice. "Stop distracting everyone, please, or I will have to ask you to leave."

I look over at the stage and my class are all staring at me. None of them are finding it funny. Tilly is crying and Ethan and the rest of the boys look like they are going to punch me. They have been rehearsing this show for weeks, and now I have turned it into a fart festival. I get hot faced and red and shout, "Sorry," before getting up and running out of the hall.

*

After the leavers' play I manage to sit still and just spin my fidget spinner in my pocket for the whole of the afternoon movie. I normally can't sit through an entire film, but after what happened in assembly I think I'd better not ask to go and roll down the hill. I don't want to remind Mrs Wheatley of my existence. Then maybe she will forget to call my mum and I'll get to go on the first holiday I've been on in years.

So I jiggle and spin and stay in the classroom for the whole afternoon and now finally I'm free. I can forget all about school. I try not to let thoughts of Redbrook enter my brain. I don't want to think about teachers or classrooms or mean faces for six whole weeks. Anyway, six weeks is a long time, maybe something will happen that will make me cool and interesting and make everyone at Redbrook want to be my friend. I might have a growth spurt and grow a moustache. I might learn how to do a backflip and dunk a basketball. I might become famous. Anything can happen in six weeks!

I run all the way home. Leaving everyone else to cry and hug and say how much they'll miss primary school. No one wants to hug me anyway. I need to find out if they called Mum. All I care about is going to Trontin's. As I let my body fly down the hill towards home my brain feels stiller than I have felt all day. The air swooshes past my face, and I throw my arms out as though I'm flying.

Mum lets me come home on my own now. She says it will get me ready for secondary school. She used to walk to school for no reason anyway, as I would just run home without her and then have to stand at the locked front door waiting for her and the Squealers to catch up.

When I get home I look through the glass in the door to see Mum alone in the kitchen and the Squealers all snuggled on the chair watching something on the computer. It looks calm and quiet. I open the door and as I throw my bag on the floor I trip over my laces and fall into the kitchen.

"And he's home!" Mum laughs. This is a good sign. If I'm making her laugh that means she is not angry which must mean she doesn't know about assembly.

"Did you book Trontin's?" I ask, unable to hold it in.

"Did you behave?"

"Yeah?" I say cautiously.

"Come here, kid," she says with a sigh which I don't fully understand the meaning of. She puts her arm around me and leads me into the living room, sitting down on the sofa.

"Listen, Reg. I just wanted to say that I'm sorry for being so…"

There is a pause while she tries to find the words, so when some options pop into my head they immediately come out of my mouth.

"Tired? Grumpy? Old?" I ask.

"Yeah," she says. "I've found it a bit tough without your dad or Kai, and I realize that I have been taking it out on you a bit. I know you can't help getting into trouble. I should be helping you, not bribing you with the promise of a holiday if you stop wriggling for a day. Wriggling is who you are."

I smile and do an over-the-top wriggle to make her laugh.

"So, I don't care what happened today at school. I don't care if you needed to roll down the hill or shout out all the answers. I've booked us two nights at Trontin's because we deserve it."

She pulls me into a cuddle and I ball my fists in celebration.

"My baby has finished primary school!" she says.

"When are we going?" I ask.

"Well, that's the thing. They had a cancellation, so pack your bags – we're off tomorrow!"

DO TRY THIS AT HOME!

HIGH FIVE!

Next time you do a high five remember to look at their elbow. You'll never miss a high five and look like a twerp again.

CHAPTER FOUR

HOLIDAY HOLIDAY HOLIDAY!!

Don't forget to pack:

- Lucky pants

- Goggles

- Cards to thrash Mum at poo head

- Miniature back scratcher

  and clothes!

There are a few things that make my mind a bit less busy or buzzy or fuzzy or wuzzy. Things that make it clearer and emptier. Running and rolling. Riding my bike. Swimming underwater and swinging high on a swing. I can do every single one of these at Trontin's!

As we arrive I see the large dome of the swimming pool with tube slides popping out of the side and vanishing back in again. There are families whizzing about on bikes and playgrounds with rope swings and tree houses. It is perfect.

The lady who gives us the keys to our cabin smiles and scrunches her nose at me, and then hands me a brochure.

"In there is a map so you can find your way around, and a list of activities and entertainment. Dinner is served from five until nine, and tonight's entertainment starts in the theatre at eight thirty – a hypnotist and mind-control expert. He's a big hit at Trontin's, so don't miss it!" She scrunches her nose again.

"What time is the pool open until?" I ask.

"The pool is open between seven a.m. and seven p.m."

"That's where I'll be then!" I say to Mum, grinning. "Can I go now?"

"Let's get to the room first, Reg."

On the way to the cabin, as Mum pulls the big suitcase along the path, I flick through the brochure, looking at all the happy faces of families and big groups laughing, playing bowls or watching a show.

"What's mind control, Mum?" I ask as I turn the page.

"I think it's just another term for hypnosis."

"What's hypnosis?"

"It's where someone talks to you and can make you do things."

"That sounds weird. Could a hypnotist control *my* mind?"

"I doubt it, Reg. No one could control your mind! Look, this is us." Mum points to a row of little wooden buildings and ours is Number 713. As we look on all the doors for the right number, a group of kids about my age speeds past us, a couple of them on bikes. They have towels and inflatables under their arms and one of them is wearing swimming goggles. They look like they are having the best time. They are laughing with each other and chatting and barely notice us. I try to smile and wave at them. I want to run with them, chase after them. To jump on the back of a bike and join in with their fun. I need to go to the pool as soon as possible and find them.

"There it is. 713. Remember that number, Reggie.

You need to get your bearings and figure out where everything is so you can find your way back. I don't mind you going off on your own, as long as you know how to get back here. All of these rooms look exactly the same."

"No, they don't. This row has a different-coloured roof. Anyway, I've memorized the map." I grin and turn the brochure around to show her the map. "The pool is over there, the restaurant is that way and the big playground is over there somewhere."

As I point out all the buildings, Mum looks confused. She is terrible at directions and always gets lost. She's always saying things like "I need to find my bearings," and "There should be more signs!" I'm good with directions though. When I was younger I got a bit obsessed with maps and floor plans. I used to build them with my Lego. A plan of school with little Lego teachers in it or our bit of town with little Lego trees and people walking down the street with a Lego dog. I like the feeling of Lego bricks clicking together. I look at the little row of cabins and the paths up to them and imagine it all in Lego.

As soon as the door is open, I rush in and am back in the living room in my swimming shorts and goggles in about one minute.

"Wow. I haven't even sat down yet, Reg."

"Can I go?"

Mum sighs as though I've done something annoying, but I don't know what, so I ask again.

"Can I go to the pool?"

"Where will I meet you? I don't know my way around yet, Reg."

"I've got my phone. When I get out of the pool I'll call and see where you are, OK?"

I can see that she's thinking about not letting me, so I push my bottom lip out and drop to my knees, holding my hands in prayer.

"OK, fine, but be safe. When I've settled in and had a cup of tea, I will come to the pool if you haven't called."

"Yes! You are the best. This will be the best holiday ever… I can feel it!"

I see the group of kids as soon as I walk into the pool. They are queuing for the big slide and leaning over the side of the stairs, shouting the word "echo" into the open space, trying to make their voices answer them back. As I watch them I want to hear the sound of my own voice and before I can stop myself I shout loudly, "Echo."

I look out into the vast dome above me and enjoy

the sound as it faintly repeats. So I shout again. And again.

When I eventually bring my gaze down from the ceiling, the kids are at the bottom of the slide and all standing on the edge of the pool staring at me. I smile back at them. They could be my holiday gang. Then Mum can have her relaxing holiday without me and I can practise not being annoying and making friends before I go to Redbrook. I wave at them, trying not to let my body be too busy.

"It's a good echo, isn't it? My name's Reggie. Are you going on again?" I ask, pointing to the slide. They don't answer and turn and head towards the lazy river so I follow.

We all get in a rubber ring and slowly float our way around the looping water. A couple of the boys start splashing each other and then wrestle until the rings flip them out and they are dunked under. It looks fun, so when they climb back into their rings I paddle my way towards them and splash water into the bigger boy's face. Just as it's about to hit him, he opens his mouth and inhales the water, coughing and choking in his rubber ring.

"Sorry!" I say, hoping that he'll stop choking and start to wrestle me like he did the other boy.

35

"Who are you?" asks one of the girls as she floats past.

"Reggie," I say, not taking my eyes off the choking boy.

"Why are you here?" says another girl.

"I won a raffle," I say.

Then the boy who I splashed finally stops coughing. "No, why are you HERE?" he says, gesturing to the group of kids who are all looking at me now from their rings.

I know these faces. I know how this works. I smile sadly and get out of my ring and head towards the slide alone. When I stop and look back to the group they are splashing and laughing and shouting, "Echo!" I'm not sure how I manage to mess absolutely everything up; I was only doing what they were doing. Why is it so hard? I don't think I will ever know how to get it right. Definitely not in time for Redbrook anyway.

Then I look up to the huge slide. I smile and sigh, shaking off any sad feelings. I'm on holiday! I don't want to be in the boring old lazy river anyway, not when I can whizz down a slide as many times as I like.

I stay in the pool, going up and down the big slide again and again. I'm still there with wrinkly fingers and slightly blue lips when I see Mum standing at the edge, waving me over.

"You have been in here for two hours, Reg!"

"I love it, Mum. The slide is awesome."

"Well, we need to eat tea."

"Can you bring me a sandwich and I can just stay here?"

"No! Five more minutes and then out! I've brought your clothes. I'm not sure how you thought you would get back to the room in your wet trunks."

I've stopped listening and am making my way to the steps for one last slide, edging and darting around people to get up there quicker. I can see that it's getting darker outside and there are fewer people in the pool now to when I arrived and there is no sign of the holiday kids. Maybe I will be able to hang out with them later.

I had no idea that I had been here for two hours. Sometimes that happens when I get really into something. Time can vanish. Mum calls it something like uber-focus, or hyper-focus, or something. It means that when I do something I like, I forget about everything else. She says she just wishes I would occasionally get it about schoolwork or tidying up or something useful.

"Can I come back after tea?" I ask as I'm towelling off on the side.

"No, it will be closed, but you can come back tomorrow. Let's go and eat. I'm hungry so you must be ravenous."

As she says the words my tummy gurgles and we both giggle as I start to feel the kind of hunger you only get after swimming. The kind of hunger that sends you into a rage. The kind of hunger that makes you eat like a disgusting animal when you finally get to a plate of food. Which is exactly what I do when I sit down with my plate full of buffet food.

"Delightful, Reggie," Mum says as I shovel more chips into my face.

As the hunger subsides, I hear cheering and clapping from somewhere else in the building. The sound of that, along with the noise of the clinking plates and cutlery, is busy and distracting and I want them all to stop until I have finished my food. It doesn't stop and when a huge wave of laughter erupts from the hidden room, I can't carry on shovelling in chips.

"What's that noise, Mum?"

"I think the theatre is next door, through that door. There is a show on, we can—"

But before she's finished, I'm up and walking towards the door she pointed to. As I make my way towards the sounds of laughter and peer through the door, I see a strange sight. Two grown men and an older lady are standing on the stage, flapping their folded arms and clucking like chickens. The audience are howling with laughter. Mum arrives behind me and puts my plate of food in front of me.

"Weird, isn't it?" she whispers.

"What are they doing?"

"They've been hypnotized."

"But if you could control minds, why would you make people turn into chickens?"

"Because it's funny, I guess. What would you do if you could control minds?" She says it casually, but the words sound loud and clear in my head and I repeat them over and over to myself.

What would you do if you could control minds?
What would you do if you could control minds?
What would you do if you could control minds?

The first thing that buzzes into my brain is a flood of ideas about how I could hypnotize people into being my friends at Redbrook. I could find my very own gang. I could make people smile at me instead of frown. I could make the teachers give me prizes for shouting the answers out instead of telling me off. But then I think of something even better. Maybe instead of hypnotizing people into liking me, maybe I could change everyone else so they all became like me? I could have a whole class of people who can't put their bottoms on the chairs. I could have a teacher who can't concentrate in a busy room. I could make everyone stay awake all night with a busy brain. Maybe if everyone else knew what it was like to be me, they wouldn't be so cross all the time.

I shovel in the last of my chips and go into the theatre, sliding into an empty seat at the end of a row. As I sit down and focus on the stage, I see the hypnotist and feel a buzz of excitement.

DO TRY THIS AT HOME!

MIND-READING POST-IT

You need a Post-it note for this. Draw a circle in the centre of the Post-it note. Make it quite small so that it doesn't come out to the edges but big enough to clearly write a word inside. Now tell your volunteer that the circle is your crystal ball and anything inside you will be able to see in your mind's eye. Now ask them to write a word in the circle and then tell them to fold it in half and in half again so that the paper is now in quarters. Take the Post-it and tear it up but keep the folded inner corner safe, and when you have ripped the edges off into small pieces, pass them back to your victim — sorry, volunteer. They will not notice you have kept the important corner piece to yourself and

will think that they have the entire
Post-it in torn-up pieces in their hand.
Now ask them to eat it! As they chew
on the paper you can secretly unfold
the corner in your hand. When they
rightly refuse to swallow the paper
you can laugh and tell them they
can put it in the bin. As they do this,
snatch a glance at the unfolded corner.
On it you will see their word inside
the circle. Now you can go to town
asking them to send the word to you
through the air and you can reveal it
however dramatically you wish. This
is a great trick and they will never
guess how you did it. Enjoy!

CHAPTER FIVE

TRY NOT TO FORGET PEOPLE'S NAMES!

When someone tells you their name, repeat it and make a comment about it, and then you are more likely to remember it.

Remember when you forgot Auntie Clare's name, she looked like she might cry and she only sent a fiver in the post that Christmas.

"Five, four, three, two, one, and you are awake and back in the room." The lady who, five minutes ago, was clucking and flapping her wings, opens her eyes and blinks a few times. She looks dazed and a bit embarrassed, but when he tells her to stand

43

and take a bow she does and the audience whoop and cheer.

"What a wonderful chicken you were. Now you can make your way back to your seat." He guides her off the stage and turns to the audience with a smile. He is in total control, everyone waiting to see what will happen next. There are so many tricks, ideas and things that I need to remember. I've never been so still in my life. He takes a drink of water and then looks out to the crowd.

"Stand up if you had the same breakfast this morning as you did yesterday."

Most people in the audience stand up, including me. I have Shreddies every single morning. I love them. There is shuffling and giggling in the audience as we wonder what's about to happen. I see the holiday kids all run down the aisle and out of the side door. They look like they are playing tag or hide-and-seek. Normally I would run after them and join in, but I'm rooted to the spot, hanging on the hypnotist's every word.

"Stay standing if you will probably have the same thing again tomorrow." A couple of people sit down. I stand, looking around. More giggling.

"Stay standing if you believe that someone can be hypnotized."

Lots of people sit. I stay standing. I believe it; why else would they have been chickens? More laughter. Then he looks towards the doors and says, "Right, very good, everyone. Don't be nervous, it's not like I make anyone look silly, is it?! OK, everybody who is standing, turn and face either wall. Right or left, it doesn't matter." I turn to the right.

"Sit down if you turned to the left." There are just a few of us left now. My heart beats faster. I don't know what is happening but I want to be here until the end. I want to keep standing so that he can see me.

"Stay standing if you had not noticed the elephant in the room."

Everyone laughs at this, and most people sit down. I look around, wondering what everyone is laughing at. Mum nudges me and points to a huge blow-up elephant that is wafting around at the front of the room. I'm not sure how I missed it, but I did, so I stay standing. It's just me and two other people now. I feel giddy, like I might be sick.

"OK, so the next section of the show is all about luck. As you will see, our wonderful elephant here has his trunk pointing up in the air, which to many people means it's lucky. I will prove on this stage tonight that there is no such thing as luck. Of the last standing, who thinks they are lucky? Who has won something or found something in the last week?"

My arm shoots into the air and before I can stop myself, I shout, "I won this holiday! I won this holiday!" The hypnotist smiles.

"Well, it looks like we have a volunteer!"

Mum has got her head in her hands. She thinks I'm going to embarrass myself. Embarrass her. But I'm not. For the first time in my life, I feel like I'm meant to be here. I feel totally relaxed as I step up on to the stage. I can't wait to see what happens. I had no idea that it was possible to control people's minds. If I had known this years ago I would be the world's best hypnotist by now.

"Welcome to the stage, young man. What is your name?"

"Reggie. What's yours?"

"My name is Michael Gareth."

"Michael Gareth. That's two first names."

"Very astute, Reggie. Please take a seat."

I sit down and keep my eyes fixed on him. I want to see what he is doing, to learn everything I can from him.

"So, Reggie, please confirm for the audience that you are not an actor, we have never met before today and that you came on to the stage out of choice; no one forced you to come up here."

I nod my head. I can feel my heart beating inside my neck. It feels like it might burst through my skull.

"So, Reggie, you think you are lucky?"

"Well, I was lucky to win the tickets and I'm lucky to be here, so yeah."

"Lovely. So innocent. So sweet. I am about to ruin all of that wonderful childish hope and show you that there is no such thing as luck. In front of you I will place three boxes." I watch hard as he puts down three small cardboard boxes on to a table and taps the top of each of them. I try hard to focus and check if he is doing anything else. Anything that might hypnotize me or that I might not spot.

"There is twenty pounds inside one of these boxes, Reggie. Would you like twenty pounds?"

"Yeah!" I say, instantly wondering what I would buy with it.

"It's yours, dear boy. All you have to do is pick which box it's in. One, two or three."

I look at the boxes and then look out at Mum who

47

is smiling. I'm about to say box number one and Michael Gareth smiles.

"Now, I don't want to confuse you, but most people go for box one…"

How did he know?!

"So, as most people go for that, I will give you a little clue. I know that people go for the first box and so I say it out loud to make you change your mind."

I glance at the other boxes and then he describes almost exactly what is going on inside my head.

"Your mind will skip to box two and then try to outsmart me by landing on box three. When I ask for your answer, you will sigh and not know whether to stick on box three or twist and move to box two. Then your brain will say, 'Hang on a minute, maybe all this is a trick and the money IS in box number one.' So, Reggie, it's decision time. Which box is it in?"

I feel so confused and lost, not knowing which box to pick. I feel like he has put me off all of them.

"Two?" I say.

"Number two. You are wrong, of course." He opens the empty box and shows everyone that it is empty. "So now you have box one and box three. What is it to be?"

"Three," I say quickly before he can baffle me with more words.

"Three. Are you sure? You can change your mind. Now, would I let you change your mind if you had got it wrong? Why would I do that? Am I trying to control you?" He is so calm. It almost makes me dizzy how calm he is. I panic as my mind skips between the boxes and he just smiles as though he can see my thoughts.

"I would always change my mind. But I am me, and you are you. Would you like to change your mind? Most people stick, but what would you do?"

My mind freezes, not knowing what to do. He is confusing me, and I know that whatever I choose will be wrong. It's like he knows me better than I know myself. I go from three to one again and again and then say, "I'll stick with three."

"What a shame," he says as he opens the empty box number three and then shows us what's inside box one. A small elephant with its trunk in the air wrapped in a twenty-pound note.

"Now that could just be luck. Bad luck, in this case – for you. Shall we try it again just to check?"

After picking the wrong boxes five more times and being completely bamboozled by Michael Gareth's words, I know that he could make me do anything.

When I leave the stage holding the lucky elephant and no twenty-pound note I know that I HAVE to learn how to do this. I need to meet Michael Gareth and find out how to control people's minds.

DO TRY THIS AT HOME!

TOO TIRED TO CARRY
YOUR OWN STUFF?

Next time you are carrying something
and don't want to, just keep talking
as you hold out the item to the other
person. They should automatically
take it from you, as they don't want to
interrupt what you're saying. Either
that or they will call you a lazy turd,
but it's worth a try.

CHAPTER SIX

WRITE STUFF DOWN!

If you get giddy and can't remember everything that someone is saying, write it down.

Remember that time Mum told you the things you needed to get from the shop, and you told her you were definitely listening? Then you got to the shop and realized that actually you'd been thinking about the slightly cheesy smell that was coming from your feet.

I watch silently and in total stillness as Michael Gareth continues the show. He reads people's minds, draws pictures of exactly what they are thinking, convinces them that they are related to complete strangers, and hypnotizes them into putting their wallet, keys and phones into a charity bucket. At the end, when everyone is cheering and he is giving back the confused volunteers their belongings, I'm up on my feet, clapping until my hands hurt.

"Thank you, thank you, and remember, ladies and gentlemen, know your own mind. I will be here tomorrow lunchtime doing some close-up magic. Come and join me. Until then, goodbye." With that he winks and leaves the stage.

I turn to Mum. "I have to meet him! I'll find you in the bar, OK?" She smiles and nods her head. She will think that this is another one of my phases. Like when I got fixated on learning how to skateboard and kept breaking my bones, or the time I wanted to become an astronaut and wouldn't get out of my spacesuit for three weeks. (In the end she made me take it off because it stank and she thought I would pass out from the fumes.) This is not like that though. I was a kid back then, I had no idea how to skateboard or get into space. This is something that I can actually learn. I'm old enough. I can read and practise and figure out how to hypnotize people. The best thing

53

is that I have a whole six weeks to do it before I start school. If I can do this everyone will want to be my friend. I dash down the aisle, towards the curtain where Michael Gareth vanished.

Maybe I could change my name and have two first names too. Reggie Sam or Harry Reggie. They don't sound very good. Maybe Reggie Houser is good enough. I will ask Michael Gareth when I meet him. After a few minutes of waiting for him to come back out through the curtain I have a moment of panic when I realize there might be a back door he can sneak out, away from all his adoring fans.

The theatre is almost empty now apart from me and an old man asleep in the third row with a half-empty pint of beer in his hand. I half wonder if he's been accidentally hypnotized, until a woman in leggings and flip-flops stomps up the aisle and shakes him.

"Dad. Wake up, you old soak. Dad!"

He snorts and nearly spills the rest of his drink, and she leads him out of the room so that it's just me waiting by the curtain.

I can't wait any longer so I have a peek through the gap and see Michael Gareth sitting on the other side slouched in a chair, rubbing his forehead with his hands.

"Excuse me," I say quietly. He jumps at the sound of my voice.

"You scared me! What you doing back here, kid? The show's over."

"I want to know how to do it," I say.

Michael Gareth sighs. "Which one, kid?"

"All of it. I want to control people's minds."

He laughs in a sad way and shakes his head.

"I wouldn't waste your time, kid. There is no money in hypnosis these days, unless you're happy to live your life on cruise ships and in holiday parks."

"Living on cruise ships and in holiday parks sounds amazing!" I say, wondering why Michael Gareth looks so tired and sad when he is not on stage.

"Yeah, that's what I thought when I started." There is a pause where I'm not sure what to say, and he looks at me and it's like he shakes off whatever the sad thoughts are in his head and smiles.

"Reggie? The boxes?"

"Yeah," I say.

"And now you want to learn how I did it?"

"Yeah."

"Why? Why do you want to learn?" He looks serious as he asks me this question. I think about it and I am about to say because I want people to like me, but then I think a bit more.

"Because I'm different to everyone else. My mind works differently. I want to understand people's minds. I want to make friends."

"Wow. That's an answer, kid. Normally the ones who wait after the show just want to learn how to trick people into doing silly things. They want a shortcut but it's not easy. It takes time."

"I want to learn," I say.

"OK, Reggie." He throws me a pen and a pad of paper. "Write down everything I'm about to tell you." I catch the pen and smile up at him.

"Let's start with books…"

Michael Gareth then lists all of the books, websites and people I need to look up. He tells me the first things that I need to practise, and warns me that not everyone can be hypnotized.

"You have to pick people carefully. The way I chose you. I knew you were suggestible from the questions I asked. You were still standing which meant that you were one of the most suggestible people in the room. If I had picked just anyone they might have chosen different boxes and ruined the show."

"What does suggestible mean?" I ask.

"It means that you are more likely to go along with what someone suggests."

"Is it a good thing?"

"Well, it's a good thing if you want to be part of a show about mind control, but in real life, you have to be careful. You have to know your own mind, Reggie. Don't let people around you control it." I know all about my mind. I have answered questions and talked to doctors and had my mind all figured out. It's other people's minds I have a problem with. Michael Gareth starts zipping his bag up.

"Right, I've got to go. I have to get to Brigmouth for a gig at an eightieth birthday party. Let's just hope no one in the audience karks it before the end of the show. Good luck, Reggie. I hope you figure out what you need to figure out."

As he stands to go, I hold out the pen and he shakes his head. "Keep it, kid."

As he walks through the curtain, I look down at the pen; on it are the words: *Know your own mind, Michael Gareth.*

DO TRY THIS AT HOME!

OPTIONS

Give someone options. Instead of
asking your Auntie Maureen if you are
allowed something from the shop say:
"Auntie Maureen, could I get a Twix or
a bag of sweets from the shop?"
She will then pick one and you are in!
Thanks, Auntie Maureen.

CHAPTER SEVEN

REMEMBER!!!

Take pants to the swimming pool to change into or Mum will call you a "pantless wonder" again, which is weird and embarrassing.

"There is no way that I'm letting you hypnotize me, Reggie!"

"Please!"

"No, I'm reading my book. I thought you wanted to go swimming all day?"

"I've changed my mind. Just five minutes. Please? I can't try it out on myself," I whine.

I spent the whole night hiding under the covers

looking at all of the websites Michael Gareth told me about. I've watched YouTube videos on how to do it and have written down so many cool ideas to try. I have to get started straight away or it feels like my brain will explode.

Normally, Mum makes sure I don't have any screens in my room at night. I find it hard enough to sleep anyway and she thinks screens make it worse. But because we're on holiday she forgot our normal rules and I snuck my phone into bed and stayed up all night.

Now I know loads of new stuff. Induction is the way you send someone into hypnosis; there are loads of different methods and I want to try them all. REM stands for Rapid Eye Movement and happens when someone is in a trance. Misdirection is when you guide someone to look at or think about the wrong thing. And suggestion is when you plant an idea in someone's head. They are all super cool and interesting.

The thing I want to try on Mum is a really basic hypnosis but it says you can't just do it to someone, they have to be up for it, you have to get their permission. Judging by Mum's grumpy face as she closes her book, she's not really into the idea of being hypnotized, but she's all I've got.

"Fine," she eventually says, when she can't bear me staring at her any more.

"OK, lie down on the sofa," I say.

"Well, I can manage that."

"Do I have your permission to hypnotize you?" I say, secretly re-reading the instructions from my phone.

"Yes!"

"Close your eyes and roll your eyeballs back into your head," I say.

"That doesn't sound very relaxing," she moans, but I can see her eyes rolling upwards and her eyelids begin to flutter like it says on the website. I quickly read the next step: *Focus on deepening your client's trance. For example, repeat relaxing phrases in a smooth, melodic voice.*

I try to think of something but nothing calm or relaxing comes to mind. I look out of the window and try to make my voice sound smooth and melodic.

"The sky is grey and it's a little bit windy."

Mum's eyes pop open. "What are you trying to do? Hypnotize me into becoming a weather woman?"

"Shhh, close your eyes again. I'm being relaxing!" I say. She smirks and closes her eyes.

After five minutes of me describing what I can see

in the room in a melodic voice, Mum is crying with laughter and clearly not hypnotized.

"Stop laughing. It's not funny," I say. I really want to do this. I don't think she gets it. It's important. If I can learn how to do this everything will change. Redbrook will be amazing. I will be the most popular kid in the school and I will find the best gang of mates ever. But none of that will happen if Mum keeps giggling.

"Sorry, love. Maybe I'm one of those people who just can't be hypnotized."

Maybe she's right. Maybe I should go and find someone else to try it on.

"Either that or you might need to work on your relaxing chat. Think more warm sunny beaches and less 'the door is blue, there is a kettle in the kitchen and some tea bags on the side'."

As I'm skulking back into my room to do more research, Mum calls out, "No! I know what's happening, Reggie Houser. You are getting fixated. I know you've been up all night."

Before I can even start to answer, she carries on. "It's great that last night's show connected with you, but there is no way you are spending all day on that phone watching hypnotists. Go to the pool and take a break, please."

I'm about to argue but then I remember one of the videos I saw last night. The mind-control expert said that you can see how mind control works in the real world if you look for it carefully enough. He said there are loads of ways that human beings are controlled and manipulated in everyday life and that to become a master of suggestion, firstly you need to see it at work in the real world. I can't imagine how people will be controlled in a swimming pool but maybe I'm about to find out.

Then I remember that Michael Gareth is doing magic at lunchtime. This is perfect, I can swim and look for signs of mind control and then tell Michael all about it!

As soon as I enter the pool I see things in a different way, as though my eyes are open for the first time. Images of rules and arrows pointing to various places, directing people where to go and what to do. People all unquestioningly doing it. The lifeguard stands on the edge with his whistle occasionally giving it a quick blow to stop kids jumping in or dunking each other. When the whistle sounds, everyone in the pool looks up and stops what they are doing. Is this mind control?

I head straight to the steps and make my way up

towards the slide. My brain feels foggy after a night of no sleep. I can feel my muscles and my brain twitching. Most people have less energy when they haven't slept, but my body is a bit different and it feels like I have more.

There is a queue for the slide and as I reach the end of it, I notice that everyone ahead of me has left a one-step gap between them and the next person. Last night I saw a video about herd mentality and how human beings all want to blend in and be the same. The need to be part of the herd makes us behave in certain ways. That's probably why I want my brain to be like everyone else's or everyone else's to be like mine. I want to be part of the herd. In the video there was this cool test where they put two actors in a waiting room with a load of chairs and they stayed standing up until a bell went then they sat. When it went again, they stood up. The bell kept going and they kept sitting and standing. When they sent new people into the waiting room, who had no idea what was going on, they all just joined in with the sitting and standing even though no one had asked them to, and it made no sense at all! People kind of want to be controlled. If you can control people's minds with just a bell, imagine what else you could do. On one website it said there are loads of ways you can get groups to behave differently, you need to "Lead with confidence, clearly demonstrate the behaviours you want to see and start small".

As I turn the corner of the steps I can see the lifeguard at the top. She is waiting for the red light to turn green and then sending the next slider on their way. "One, two, three." When she has counted them in, they whoosh down the slide as though she has pressed play on a remote control. The next person waits obediently on the line on the floor. "One, two, three," she says again, sounding bored of her own voice. Then I have an idea. I'm going to try it. Try and make something happen. The next time she says, "One, two, three," I clap my hands three times afterwards like an echo of her words. A couple of people look around and I nearly lose my nerve.

"One, two, three," she says again.

Clap, clap, clap.

No one joins in. Shall I keep going? Then I remember the words "lead with confidence".

"One, two, three."

Clap, clap, clap.

Still nothing. There are six people ahead of me. Six chances to control minds. The queue behind me is long. I turn around and smile at the little kids next to me. The girl giggles and holds on to her mum's leg.

"One, two, three." I look at the little girl and clap my hands three times and I know instantly that I have got her. Next time she'll clap, I know it!

"One, two, three."

Clap, clap, clap.

She does! She lets go of her mum's leg and claps in time with me. The next time two more people join in and by the time I'm at the front of the queue everyone is clapping. I'm grinning so widely I almost don't want to go down the slide. I want to stay here and feel the magic of what I started.

As I hear the lifeguard's words, I give a salute to the clapping queue and whoosh myself down the slide, whooping as I go. I did it. I actually did it!

DO TRY THIS AT HOME!

SHAPES

Think of a shape. Like a square but
not a square. Picture it in your mind.
Really picture it. Now imagine another
shape around that one so it's sitting
inside. Imagine it clearly in your mind.
If you thought of a triangle inside
a circle, you will be like most other
people. Try it on them and use your
hands to vaguely outline the shapes
you want them to pick as you speak. If
you are too obvious you will look like
a numpty though, so keep it subtle! If
they are annoying and pick something
daft like a star inside a pentagon, then
call them a turd and run as fast as
your little legs can carry you.

CHAPTER EIGHT

If people say you are annoying, don't ask them why or follow them, or keep trying to join in. It usually makes them even more annoyed.

The theatre looks different. There are big, round tables with red tablecloths on and families sitting around drinking drinks and laughing and chatting. I scan the room and see Michael Gareth standing at a table in the corner, shuffling a pack of cards in a fancy way, the cards flying up in a high arc. I dash over to tell him about what happened at the pool, but as I get there, before I have a chance to speak, he puts a hand on my shoulder and tells me to look in my pocket. Confused by the change to my plan, I impatiently shove my hands into my pockets to find a folded-up playing card in the left-hand side. I take it out and the table of people gasp. I smile, enjoying the sound of their amazement.

"Open it up, Reggie," Michael says, and I'm secretly thrilled that he remembers my name. I open up the Queen of Hearts and the table gasps again. I have no idea what has just happened, but I love the feeling that I'm somehow part of it.

"Take a bow, Reggie," says Michael, and I do as I'm told.

"I just controlled minds in the swimming pool!" I whisper loudly as I come up from my bow.

Michael pats me on the back and says, "I have an apprentice, ladies and gentleman." They look at me and smile as I wriggle and jiggle. "Reggie, why don't you go and sit with the kids, and I will come and show you all some magic when I have finished blowing minds over here? You can tell me all about your mind control then."

I look over to where he's pointing and see the holiday kids sitting around drinking cans of coke and rolling an empty can around the table.

"OK," I say and I dash over to the table and sit in one of the empty chairs. This is my chance. I have to test my new skills on them. If I can make them like me then I know it will work at Redbrook. They stop rolling the can and all look at me. Three of the girls have colourful braids in their hair that weren't there yesterday and the boys look older somehow. It looks like they're waiting for me to say something, so I do.

"Michael Gareth says he'll come over and show us some magic."

One of the girls rolls her eyes and tuts. "I hate magic. It's so annoying."

Then another agrees. "Me too. It's basically just lying."

"I'm learning hypnosis," I say. "That's better than magic."

"What can you do?" asks one of the boys, who has a cap on and an earring in one ear. They're interested now. More interested in me than they have been before. I knew it would work. Being able to hypnotize people will make them like me, I know it. I start telling them everything I found out from last night's research. I'm getting excited and I keep forgetting what I'm talking about and changing subject, going from hypnosis to magic to mind control. I know what I want to say but it's all coming out in a babble. I can see them all rolling their eyes and smirking at each other, so I stop.

"You're weird," one of the girls says and I can feel my chance to make friends slipping away from me. I won't get many more chances like this before school starts. I won't meet new kids, kids that don't know me and that I have to impress. This is such a great opportunity.

"I could try it on you, if you like," I blurt before I can really think about what I'm saying.

As soon as I've said it, I know it's a mistake. I might have made people clap in a queue but I'm a long way from being able to do this.

"Go on, then, hypnotize her," the boy says, pointing at a girl with an orange braid.

"He's not coming anywhere near me!" she squeals. The other girls huddle round, saying I'm not allowed near any of them.

"All right then, do it to me," the boy in the cap says.

I think about all of the things I watched last night and decide to try a quick hypnosis. I don't think they will sit and wait for me to talk in a calm slow voice about what's in the room, so this is my only option.

"What's your name?"

"Keelyn."

"OK, Keelyn, press down on my hand with your

fingers," I say. He whispers something to the others, which makes them all laugh, I know it was something horrible about me but I ignore it and carry on. He puts his fingers into my palm and presses down. As he presses, I lock eyes with him and feel the moment where he may be about to give up. Before he stops pressing, I quickly take my hand away, making his body lean forward towards me. In the same moment, I click the fingers of my other hand in front of his eyes.

"Close your eyes and sleep," I say as confidently as I can. His head lolls forward instantly and it looks like it's worked. I can't quite believe it. I'm not exactly sure what to do now and so I start talking, trying to deepen the hypnosis.

"With each breath out, you will go deeper and deeper." The kids all giggle but I'm focused.

"The sounds of voices and giggles only make you go deeper into hypnosis. With every sound, you go deeper. When you wake you will forget the number seven," I say, remembering a trick I'd seen last night. "When I count down from three, your eyes will open and you will be back in the room. Three, two…" And as I'm about to say "one" the boy flicks his head up fast and shouts, "WEIRDO!" into my face.

72

I jump out of my skin and make a strange-sounding squeal which makes them all howl with laughter. He leaps out of his chair and sings, "Seven, seven, I love the number seven." My shoulders slump as the holiday kids laugh and look at me with snarky faces. I sigh and bite the inside of my cheek, feeling my throat tighten. I've failed. It didn't work on Mum and it hasn't worked on them. Maybe I will never be able to do it. Maybe I will never make a single friend in my whole life, let alone find a gang of my own at Redbrook. I don't want to go to secondary school. Not if it's going to be like this.

"As if you would ever be able to do that," Keelyn says, kicking the legs of my chair from underneath me, making me fall painfully to the floor.

"You're such a weirdo," one of the girls adds as they all get up to leave.

"Don't follow us, please."

"He's so annoying."

I watch as they walk away, feeling tears prick my eyes. If I had been able to do it, I would have been a hero. They would definitely have wanted to hang out with me if I could do it.

I nearly jump out of my skin for a second time as I feel a gentle pat on my shoulder.

"You picked the wrong kid," Michael Gareth says with a knowing smile. "That one was never going to be hypnotized, the little brute. Learning who's suggestible is just as big a skill as doing the hypnosis. You'll get there though. You've just got to work on it."

I sigh as he sits down and I get to my feet and pick up my chair, trying to stop the embarrassed tears from falling down my cheeks.

"Not easy being a kid, is it?" he says kindly.

"No, not when you seem to annoy every other kid on the planet. Everyone hates me; I don't get it."

"I was the same. Never had many friends."

"No way," I say, not believing that someone like him hadn't always been surrounded by people who loved him and were amazed by him.

"Yeah, I was a bit of a nerd." He narrows his eyes and looks at me. "I bet there is someone who likes you. There is always one friend."

"Not for me."

"Maybe you're not looking hard enough."

I feel the tears prick my eyes again and just as I'm about to describe all the scowly faces at school and about how I completely ruined the play, I see Mum. She waves and comes over to the table.

"So, it's your fault that my son was awake all night YouTubing hypnotists!"

Michael Gareth puts his hands up and says, "Guilty as charged." They both laugh and then he looks a bit more serious.

"Reggie here was telling me there is not a single kid in the entire world who likes him, and I just can't believe that's true."

Mum looks instantly sad. "No, that's not true," she says.

I stare at her, knowing that there's not one person who she can name as a friend of mine. After an awkward pause, she tries.

"What about the boy you play basketball with?"

"Mum, he throws basketballs at me."

"The girl who helped you with your maths that time?"

"Sir made her do that as a punishment for laughing at me."

Mum thinks and we sit in silence as we all deal with the reality that I literally don't have a single friend, then she gasps and perks up.

"What about Frizz?!"

"Arghh, stop going on about Frizz being my friend."

"Well, she is."

"She doesn't count," I say.

"Why on earth not? She always wants to come and hang out with you. In fact Jane said she's always asking when she will next see you. She's kind and she likes you. She's a perfect friend. You just can't see it."

"She doesn't count," I say again.

"Give me one good reason."

"She's a girl and she's weird and small. There are three. I wouldn't care if I never saw her again!" I know that Mum is furious but I keep my eyes fixed on Michael Gareth and carry on, trying to delay her response.

"She makes me play with teddies! She is babyish. It's one thing playing with her at home where no one can see, but I would never be seen dead with her outside in the real world."

"Reggie Houser, that is enough!" Mum looks really cross and I know I've gone too far. Said words that should have stayed inside my head again.

"How can you be so cruel? It's no wonder you don't have friends if that's how you treat them. You need to learn how to spot a true friend."

I look at Michael Gareth pleadingly.

"If I could do what you do, then I would find some real friends."

"Shall I teach you a couple of little tricks?" he says.

"Yes, please!" I say, instantly forgetting how bad I feel, but as I look at Mum I can tell she is still fuming. Luckily Michael Gareth saves me.

"OK, but I'm parched. Go and get me a cup of tea from the restaurant while I have a chat to your mum and then I'll teach you some stuff to wow your friends." As I'm leaving, he says, "Tell the waitress it's for me and they might give you a piece of cake as well."

As I'm carrying the tea tray back from the restaurant, with the biggest piece of chocolate cake you could imagine on it, I see Michael Gareth and Mum talking closely. It looks as though they are plotting something or sharing secrets and when they see me they sit up as though nothing is happening. I'm pleased when Mum gets up to go.

"I'll leave you two to it. Just don't come back and send me into a trance, Reggie, OK?"

When she leaves, Michael Gareth pours his tea and says, "I need to hypnotize you, Reggie."

"Will it help me to control people's minds and make friends?" I ask.

"I hope so, Reggie. I hope it will help you to find true friendship. Are you ready?"

I nod my head.

As soon as he clicks his fingers I feel my head roll forward and my eyes close. It feels strange, as though I could just choose to wake up, but I don't. It's a bit like the time I was ill and I couldn't sleep but I lay on my bed, staring at the ceiling for hours, listening to the noises downstairs but not really hearing them. That's what it's like now. I can hear Michael Gareth's voice and the noises of the room around me, but none of it feels real. He tells me that every noise will send me deeper, and it does. He tells me that I can do anything that I put my mind to and that if I really want to become a hypnotist then I can. Then he keeps talking and I drift away, not fully hearing what he is saying but somehow knowing that it's going in.

When he counts and clicks me back into the room, I feel so awake and full of energy but not the wriggly, jiggly energy from before. I feel happy.

"So, Reggie, let me ask you some questions to see whether that all worked."

"OK." I nod.

"How do you feel?"

"Great! Better than ever!" I say.

"Good, and tell me what makes a good friend."

"Someone who plays with you and isn't mean?" I ask, confused now about what exactly is happening.

"Good, and is there anyone like that in your life at the moment?"

"No," I say confidently. "Absolutely no one."

"OK, well, when you find someone like that you have to promise to look after them and tell them that they are a good friend, OK?"

"OK," I say, still unsure what's happening.

Michael Gareth drinks the last of his tea and goes to stand up then he pauses and says, "Oh yeah, and what noise does a cow make?"

"That's easy," I say, but I'm a bit confused when I open my mouth and *baa* like a sheep.

"What did you do?!" I giggle.

"That one will wear off, kid, the other stuff might take a bit longer." He laughs as he turns to leave.

"What other stuff?"

"You'll find out when you are ready."

I frown, desperately trying to remember what he said to me as he walks away.

"What about your cake? What about teaching me some tricks?" I call after him, pointing to the plate.

"The tricks are all in the books. The cake is for you." He winks. "Good luck, Reggie."

And as he leaves I try to *moo* and yet again I sound like a strange sheep.

"I definitely need to learn how to do this to people!" I say to myself before taking a huge bite out of the cake and smiling as I chew. I already feel happier and I haven't even learned how to hypnotize yet.

DO TRY THIS AT HOME!

WHISPER

Whisper something to someone and see if they whisper back. If they do, you can then whisper, "Why are we whispering?" Hopefully they will whisper, "I don't know." And you can look at them strangely as though they started the whole thing.

CHAPTER NINE

THE NEIGHBOURS' NAMES
SO YOU DON'T FORGET:

— Helena and Roger. Number 8. Always wear matching jumpers. A bit weird. They smile a lot, which kind of makes them even weirder.

— John and Deirdre. Number 22. Really old but still hold hands.

— Barry. Number 30. Never in. Drives a van.

— Mr Richards. Number 12. Looks like a head teacher. Maybe that's why everyone calls him Mr Richards instead of Bob or Fred or whatever his real name is.

"Mum?" I say, when we get back home from Trontin's.

"We have literally just walked in the door, Reggie, please don't ask something which requires me to do anything." I think about what I'm about to ask and decide that it doesn't.

"I need two audiobooks but I don't have any money." I wait for her to snap at me or shush me, but she carries on unpacking her suitcase.

"Michael Gareth gave me a list of books and I really want to listen to them." I prefer listening to books because my mind doesn't drift off as much as when I'm reading. "Two of them are on audiobook. Please could you buy them for me?"

"No, Reggie, I'm skint. You'll have to earn some money."

"How?!"

"I don't know, figure it out. If you're not going to help me with all this, can you find something to do, please? Outside."

I walk out on to the street and look up and down. Mr Richards is washing his car, and John and Deirdre are in the garden wearing hats and gardening gloves. Maybe someone will pay me to help them.

"Do you need any help?" I ask, smiling. Then I

realize it sounds like I'm just being kind, so I add, "I need to earn some money."

Mr Richards looks at me and shakes his head. "All done now. Sorry."

John and Deirdre say no as well and I almost give up when I see the new couple at Number 14 coming out of their front door. I don't know their names. The man has a baby strapped to his chest and the woman is holding the lead of a huge black Labrador who is pulling her through the door. I nearly turn away, but how on earth will I ever learn hypnosis if I can't even talk to people?

"Hi," I say as I approach them. I remember something that I read on a mind-control forum about how if you get people to say yes to three things in a row they will be more likely to say yes when you ask them to do something for you. "It's a nice day, isn't it?"

"Yes, it's lovely," the woman says, trying not to be pulled over by the dog. I desperately try to think of another yes question.

"You're new, aren't you?"

"Yes," the man says, smiling. One more yes and then I can ask.

"Is that your baby?" That makes me sound a bit ridiculous and quite dim, but they say yes and look lovingly at the baby. They don't seem to notice anything strange about the conversation. I have my three yeses and so I can ask.

"My name is Reggie. I live at Number 20."

"Nice to meet you, Reggie. I'm Dan, and this is Sarah, and this little one is Lulu."

"I'm looking for some jobs to earn some money. Do you have anything that you need help with?"

They look at each other and turn back to me. "Yes!" they say in unison. This is weird. Did I just hypnotize them both? It can't be this easy, can it? The man carries on. "We were just saying that we desperately need someone to come and let the dog out when we both go back to work."

"I can do that!" I say, looking at the dribbling hound. Not quite daring to stroke it.

"It would be from next week. Just let him into the garden for a wee and give him a bit of attention, that's all. Monday to Friday. Does twenty-five pounds a week sound OK?"

"Yes! The audiobooks I want only cost fifteen so that's amazing. I'll be able to get some others too!"

The man smiles and dashes back into the house; when he comes back out, he hands me fifteen pounds and a key.

"How about you get your books and I pay you the rest at the end of the week? Here is the key, just let yourself in. His treats and balls are in a tub by the patio doors. He will love you forever, won't you, Barnaby?" At the mention of his name the dog starts pulling even harder on the lead and sneezing wildly. I'm holding the money and the key and staring in shock at the folded-up notes. I just asked someone for money and they gave it to me. Maybe I'm going to be good at this mind-control thing.

"Ooh, just one thing," the man adds. "Don't open an umbrella in front of him. He hates them. So, if it's raining in the garden, please don't put up an umbrella."

"OK," I say, confused.

"For some reason they send him totally wild and he launches himself at them," the man explains. "The last time we went out on a rainy day, he shredded a poor old lady's brolly in front of her eyes."

"OK," I say, looking suspiciously at the huge, dribbling beast.

I've never had a dog and even though I pestered Mum to get me one for a whole year, I'm looking at Barnaby and wondering if I even like dogs, especially umbrella-eating dogs. I need the money so I try and shake off my worry and plaster a small, slightly fake smile on to my face. I wave them goodbye and try to ignore the fact that Barnaby is lurching and woofing at a squirrel across the road.

I can let a dog into a garden for ten minutes and nothing could go that wrong, could it? Anyway, at least now I can get my audiobooks! I run home clutching my cash. Everything is going to plan.

"To hypnotize someone, you have to feel confident in yourself. No one will trust your direction if you don't trust yourself."

I've barely taken my headphones off since I downloaded the books. I've already learned so much that I want to try. Mum said there is no way I am using her as a guinea pig so I need to find someone else to hypnotize.

As I take the headphones off and put the key into the lock of Number 14 on Monday, I can hear Barnaby on the other side, barking and banging around. It sounds like there is a monster on the other side of the door. I pause and wonder what to do. What if he savages me as soon as I open the door? They didn't mention anything about him having torn anyone apart before, but you never know. Barnaby could be a lot more than a big, drooling Labrador. What if he is a cold-blooded killer?

I'm about to turn around and go and ask Mum to come and protect me, but then I hear a voice coming through the headphones around my neck. As I raise them to my ears, I know what I need to do.

"*Work on your tone. Find your inner calm. Cultivate a calm and clear style. The more you practise the more confident you will become. Hypnotize the pot plants, the dishes in the sink and then you can even move on to the family pets.*"

I need to hypnotize Barnaby! The excitement I feel overwhelms the horrific sound of howling coming from inside the house and I turn the key and open the door, taking a huge breath in and finding my "inner calm". As soon as I have found my inner calm, I am hit in the chest by two huge paws and brought to the ground, Barnaby on top of me, drool falling from his jaws on to my face.

"Look into my eyes, Barnaby," I say as confidently as I can. Barnaby tilts his head and lifts his paw as though he is listening. I let him rest his paw on my hand. "You are safe. I am going to lead you on a journey. A peaceful and relaxing journey." I'm still speaking so he clearly hasn't eaten my head yet. I carry on. "Barnaby, when I click my fingers, you will lie down and close your eyes." I lift my arm from underneath Barnaby's great weight and click. There is a moment of silence when I believe that it will work. That Barnaby will be under my control. And then he licks me. He licks my entire face and covers me in doggy drool.

"Barnaby, that was not what I asked you to do, was it?" I say, wriggling free and managing to stand up and wipe my face. Maybe trying to hypnotize someone when they are pinning you to the ground is not the best way to start. But at least it got me into the house, I guess. It gave me the confidence to open the door. I laugh and give Barnaby a head rub and as soon as I do, he rolls over and lies on his back.

"Too late now, Barnaby!"

DO TRY THIS AT HOME!

SAY YES

Think of something you want to ask
for. Something that may be tricky to
get. More pocket money, a chocolate
cake the size of your face, or maybe
a worm farm. Now find your victim.
Go and ask for whatever it is you
want, and as you are asking, nod your
head. As they watch you nodding,
you can make them believe that it's a
brilliant idea. If they say yes, enjoy
your worms or cake. If they say no,
tell them they have lizard brains and
stomp out of the room like an angry
dancer.

CHAPTER TEN

Remember it's the school holidays. DO NOT put your school uniform on when you wake up!

For the next few days, in between being licked by Barnaby, I listen, watch and read everything out there about hypnosis and mind control. When I eventually fall asleep at night, I dream about people being under my spell and turning them into chickens.

At first, when Mum said she had to work all summer and that I would have to "fend for myself", I was really fed up. She said it was because we are skint and she needs to earn as much as possible to pay the bills. It didn't seem fair to me. Dad is away to earn money and Mum is here earning money and I'm left on my own all summer. But now I have my hypnosis plan it's actually worked out pretty well. I can spend all of my time learning and practising and there is no one to bother me. I still have thirty-two days until school starts. I have made a calendar for my wall so that I can tick off the days. I want to have hypnotized a real human being by then.

It's clear that Barnaby cannot be hypnotized; I have talked in my calm voice and tried out all of my new tricks and techniques and he still jumps on me and slobbers all over my face. I need a human volunteer.

This morning, as I'm looking in my mirror and trying to hypnotize myself for the hundredth time, I hear the sound of the Squealers arriving. My eyebrows lift and I smile to my reflection. Maybe I've found three little volunteers!

"Mum, what are you and the Squeal— I mean, the girls, doing today?" Mum hates it when I call them the Squealers.

Una looks up at me and sticks her tongue out so I stick mine out at her. Then Bea says, "We're going to the park! We're going to the park!"

I look at her happy little face and remember what happened in the slide queue. I bend down so that I can look into all of their wide eyes and then I repeat, "We're going to the park! We're going to the park! We're going to the park!" Every time I say the word "park" I put both my hands above my head and do a little jump. It doesn't even take a second round and they are joining in. After a minute I have them marching around the kitchen chanting and jumping in time. They are going to be easy to hypnotize!

"Yes, we are off to the park and then for a picnic."

"I'll come!" I say quickly. Maybe I can send the Squealers into a trance on the play fort.

"Don't you have to let the dog out?" she says.

"Oh yeah." My shoulders slump.

"The reality of being a working man, Reggie! We'll see you back here after."

Maybe it's a good thing. It gives me time to plan how I will hypnotize them. I can practise on Barnaby, even though he is a lost cause. It's worth another try. I really want this to work.

"Barnaby, look into my eyes." I'm holding a dog treat and drool is pouring from his mouth. He's looking at me, but then glancing at the treat. I use my best confident, calm voice and I think it sounds pretty good. I do some long blinks and am gently swaying to try and get him into a trance-like state. It's hard with Barnaby because I can't tell him to close his eyes or to copy me. I think I see him swaying slightly, and as I keep talking in low tones, I'm sure he blinks for longer than he normally would. I've tried this so many times but today something feels different. I feel calmer, more confident.

"Barnaby, when I tell you to lie down, you will roll on to the floor and keep listening to the sound of my voice." I have never known him to be this quiet. I'm not sure what's happening but it might actually be working. "You are safe and calm, you are content and warm. I am in control. Barnaby, lie down." He sways again and for a moment I think he is not going to do it and then all of a sudden, his gigantic body slumps and hits the floor. I stifle a scream of delight and keep talking in my special voice. "Barnaby, when you wake up you will no longer think that you are a dog. When you wake up you will hop instead of walk, you will croak instead of bark, you will try and catch flies instead of balls. Barnaby, when you wake up you will totally believe that you are a frog." I shuffle back to give him some space. "I will count down from three, and when I get to one, Barnaby, you will become the frog that you have always wanted to be." I see his paws twitching. "Three, two, one."

One of his eyes opens and looks around the room. The other one follows and out of nowhere his whole body leaps up from the floor and lands on all fours. Oh my god, is he a frog? I think he might actually be a frog dog. He moves his head around the room and sticks his tongue out, quickly licking his lips. Very froggy. Then after a few moments of quiet, he opens his mouth and lets out a huge burp.

"BRRRRRRRRRRRRRRRRRRHHHHHH."

"You sound like a frog! You are a frog! I turned you into a frog!"

I completely forget about everything I've learned about bringing people out of hypnosis calmly and staying focused and in control and I jump about the room shouting, "You're a frog! You're a frog! You're a frog dog." Barnaby joins in and leaps higher and higher in the air with each jump, his eyes wide. I think he looks happier as a frog than as a dog. As we are leaping and bouncing around the kitchen the front door opens and Dan and baby Lulu come through it.

"Wow! What on earth is going on?!"

I panic. What should I do? I have turned his dog into a frog. He might be cross with me.

"We are just playing a game," I say. "Pretending to be frogs."

"Interesting! Lulu has a temperature, poor little lamb. I had to get her from nursery. I need to pay you for the week now, don't I, Reggie?"

He gets his wallet out and I sneak a look at Barnaby, who shoots his tongue out after an imaginary fly.

"Here you go. Thanks so much for this week. Barnaby, have you had fun?"

He goes to stroke the dog on the head and before his hand gets there, Barnaby leaps into the air and lands perfectly on all fours on the sofa.

"I have literally never seen him do that before."

"Yeah, he got really into the game," I say, walking towards the door. "He might be a bit froggy for a while, but it should wear off." I can see Dan looking confused as he turns back to Barnaby and then looks back to me.

"Bye! See you next week. Hope Lulu gets better!" I close the door and lean my back against it, before running and laughing all the way home.

When I burst through the door the Squealers are sitting on the sofa watching their afternoon telly. I squeeze in next to them and try to lower my excited voice into a whisper so that Mum can't hear.

"I just turned the neighbours' dog into a frog!"

Bea turns and narrows her eyes. "No, you didn't," she says, turning back to the film.

"I did! I can do it to you, if you like. Do you want to be a frog?"

"No!" Bea shouts and folds her arms.

"Una, do you want to turn into a frog?"

"No, I want to be a cat," she says without taking her eyes off the movie.

"I can do that!" I whisper. Then my mum's voice sounds loudly across the kitchen.

"You can do what, Reggie? Why are you whispering?"

"He wants to turn us all into frogs," says Mabel matter-of-factly with her finger firmly inside her nostril.

"No one is turning anyone into anything, Reggie Houser. Now go and get your stuff ready. Tomorrow is the induction fun day at Redbrook."

"What?"

"You know about it. I told you."

I have absolutely no idea what she is talking about. I don't know anything about an induction fun day. She sees the blank look on my face.

"I knew you weren't listening. I read the letter out

to you after sports day, remember? It's on the fridge."
She points to the fridge and there is a letter stuck on
it with the heading in big red letters.

REDBROOK INDUCTION FUN DAY

How have I never seen that? I start to panic. I don't
want to go yet. I have thirty-two days left before I
need to go there. I have to be ready. I have to be able
to control minds or it will all go wrong. Mum carries
on as if nothing is the matter.

"It's a day of activities and games for the new Year
Sevens. So you can see the school with none of the big
kids in it. They always do it in the school holidays for
anyone who is around. It'll be fun."

I think back, trying to remember her telling me
about this. Sports day made my brain go really fuzzy.
It was too loud and busy and we were all being told to
do lots of things and not do lots of other things, and
it all got jumbled and I got told off for staring into
space at the start of the sack race. No wonder I wasn't
listening to Mum, my brain was busy and full for the
whole night afterwards.

"I don't want to go to school on a Saturday. I
definitely don't want to go to school in the holidays."

I'm not ready for this. I've hypnotized Barnaby, but I have to have hypnotized a real person before I go to Redbrook. That's the plan.

"It's only a day and it's not really school. You're doing fun stuff."

"Fun stuff like what?"

"Games and team-building activities. Go and pack a bag. A pen, paper, water bottle and spare clothes."

"Why? I'm not going to wet myself." She laughs at this and points to the door. I'll have to hypnotize the Squealers on Monday. I don't really want to wait that long though. I know that I can do it now. I've done it on Barnaby so I know it's possible. Then a thought hits me. Maybe I can practise on someone tomorrow. If it works, it might be a good way to make some new friends before I even start school. To find my new gang.

DO TRY THIS AT HOME!

ARM FLOAT

Stand inside a doorway and press the backs of your hands against the frame with your arms straight. Now push, as if you are trying to widen the doorway. Keep going as hard as you can for 30–60 seconds and then stop and let your arms down. You will see them magically floating up into the air.

CHAPTER ELEVEN

WASH YOUR FACE!

Remember the time you drew a fake moustache on with felt tip. That will not be a good first impression at Redbrook.

The school is massive. It looks even bigger without the swarms of kids around it like the last time I was here. We came for a "taster day" last term and every inch of playground and corridor seemed to be full of giants. Now it's eerily empty, just with a few groups of scared-looking Year Six kids heading towards the oversized main doors.

I see two boys with spray-painted hair the minute I walk into the hall. The coloured scalps drawing my eyes to their red and blue heads. One of them is throwing crisps into a girl's hood in front of him and the other is looking down at his phone. I hear someone ask one of them why their hair is dyed.

"I'm United, he's City," says the red-headed boy, gesturing to the boy on the phone. "We're twins." Then he carries on throwing crisps, until the girl in front turns and scowls at him, which makes him hoot with laughter and shove the crisp packet in her face.

The hall slowly fills up until it is humming with nervous chatter and giggles. I try to stay calm and not let my brain get too busy or my body tap or jiggle too much. I try and spot kids from my class and give them a little wave when I do. A couple of them wave back, but most of them either don't see me or pretend not to. I squish down the feelings of panic that everyone will hate me. It's going to be different here. I am a hypnotist now after all. A small, weird girl with a Hello Kitty bag waves at me from the other side of the hall, but I have no idea who she is so I pretend I haven't seen. She is definitely not the type of person I want in my gang.

The head teacher comes into the hall and talks about what we are going to do all day. I can't take my eyes off the twins though. They don't listen to anything he says, they just talk and laugh and look down at the phone. It's like they're in their own bubble. They don't seem to care about getting into trouble. At least when I get into trouble, I don't mean it and I feel bad after. I don't think they would feel bad at all. They kind of scare me as I know they are the kind of kids who could be really mean to me, but they are also the kids I want on my side. The kind of kids I want to hypnotize and become best friends with. Kids like that are only scary when you are on the outside looking in. They wouldn't scare me if I was one of them.

First, we do some team building in the hall where a man shouts lots of things at us and tells us to get across the room in groups of three without touching the floor. We can only use a chair and a tiny piece of carpet. I know exactly how to do it but as I try to explain to my team, I can hear all the noise of the other groups and it distracts me so I stop talking. By the end of the session I have gone to the corner of the room on my own and am trying to hypnotize myself instead of joining in with the noisy games. I can't even focus on watching the groups and deciding which would be the best group to try and be friends with or which kids look like the best ones to hypnotize. It's too busy to think about any of that stuff so I just sit on my own and count my breaths. I wish I had brought my plastic Spider-Man to whisper things to. I had forgotten just how hard school is.

Next, we do orienteering on the field and then it's lunch, where we all sit in the playground with our lunch boxes. As I find a sunny spot and take out my cheese butty, I see the hair-twin boys whispering and sneaking towards the gate. I'm fascinated by them; they are so wild and confident. They don't care what anyone thinks. I want to be more like them. I look around to check that no one is watching me and I follow to see where they are heading.

At the main gate there are two older boys, both with sprayed hair too, sitting on bikes and leaning against the railings. I wish my hair was sprayed a colour, even though I don't support City or United. I stay back so that they don't catch me looking at them.

"How's it going, Vince, my little buddy? Have they suspended you yet?" says the larger of the two bike boys. The crisp thrower laughs and shakes his head, slapping him hard on the back. "Not yet, but I can still beat your record."

They all laugh and chat and talk in voices that are too quiet for me to hear. I sneak a little closer, hiding behind a sign, but as I shove the last of my cheese sandwich into my mouth, I lose hold of my lunch box and it clatters to the floor. I freeze and then slowly bend to pick it up. As I raise my head I see two shaved red heads followed by two blue ones pop around either side of the sign.

"What the hell are you doing, you little weirdo?" says one of the older boys.

"Are you spying on us?" adds the blue-haired phone boy.

"No," I say quickly. "I love your hair," I add, realizing as I say it how feeble it sounds.

"Ooh, he loves our hair, boys! How sweet." Then, as he's laughing, the older red-headed boy grabs me by the back of my neck and squeezes so hard that I yelp. "Listen, you little runt. If I catch you listening in on a private conversation again, I will kill you. OK? If Vince here, or Oscar, tells me that you have been annoying them in any way at all, I will also kill you. Understood?"

I try to nod but he has hold of my neck so tightly that I can't move. My brain goes so buzzy a thousand thoughts and sounds fill my head all at the same time.

Why did I follow them?

The sounds of screaming in the playground.

How do I always get everything so wrong?
A football hitting a fence.
This is the worst way to start Redbrook.
His fingers tighten on the back of my neck.
Everything will just get even worse in September.
A siren on the main road.
I don't want to come to Redbrook.

Then, when I think I might pop, I just close my eyes and wait for it all to stop.

"What's your name, runt boy?"

"Reggie," I squeak, trying not to cry.

"Reggie what?"

"Reggie Houser."

"Well, Reggie Houser, give me one good reason why I should let go of your scrawny little neck."

I panic and try and think of something to say, anything that will make him let go and then out of nowhere I shout, "I can hypnotize people. I could turn you into chickens."

I slowly feel his grip loosen as he laughs and the others all start howling too.

"I have got to see this," says the younger one, who I assume is Oscar. They all circle me and my mind is going into overdrive. What am I going to do? It probably won't work. After all, I have only successfully managed to hypnotize a dog, and even that could have been a fluke. As they get closer, I see their faces and wonder if I really could hypnotize them. I look at their angry, laughing eyes and mean mouths and wonder if it's possible to hypnotize someone into being kinder.

"OK, then, Reggie Houser, prove it. Hypnotize Max." The older red head gets shoved towards me, but before I can even think about where to start, I hear a loud voice, which is clearly directed at us.

"WHAT IS GOING ON HERE?"

I turn to see the head teacher glaring at us. He marches our way and then looks past me and stares directly at the older boys.

"Blane, Max, I want you off school property now, please."

"Sir, we were just bringing our cousins some lunch."

"Well, they have it, so now you can leave. We have one more year of your wonderful company from September, so let's not ruin it before it even begins."

The head teacher looks at me and the two younger boys.

"Names, please."

They don't say anything and so I say, "Reggie Houser, sir."

"You two?"

"Oscar."

"Vince."

They mumble so quietly I can hardly hear them.

"You're all part of the same family, are you?"

Oscar pipes up at this suggestion. "He's not, sir." He points at me. A weird part of me feels sad when he says this. There is a part of me that would love to shave my head and dye it and have cousins to protect me, even if they were mean and terrifying.

"Well, I'm watching you. Now get back to the playground."

As we walk away from the gate, I hear one of them shout after us. "See you in September, Reggie. You'd better show us your skills then."

When I get home Mum is talking on the phone. I put my bag down and am heading upstairs to re-read my favourite hypnosis book, *Hypnotize Your Way to Happiness*. I really need to up my game and work even harder before school starts. Maybe if I hypnotize Blane and Max, they'll let me be part of their gang. Even if they don't, at least they might not grab me by the neck again. There was no chance to practise in the afternoon. We all sat in hot classrooms and did quizzes. I got really bored and had to try my hardest not to get up and walk around or shout things out.

Just as I get to the top of the stairs, Mum's voice calls after me. "It's your dad, Reg. Come and talk to him."

I run back down the stairs and take the phone. "Hi, Dad!"

"Hi, Reggie, how you doing, kid?"

"I'm OK, how are you?"

"Good. I'm coming home in a few weeks. I should be back just after you start school." My heart sinks.

"I thought you were back next week?" As I hold the phone to my ear I realize how much I need Dad to come home. The house feels different when Dad's in it. Busier and messier and louder, but better. He doesn't look at me like I am a disappointment in the way that Mum does. I think somehow he just gets me, in a way that no one else really does.

"Yeah, the job is taking more time than we thought. It won't be too much longer though. How was today? Make any new mates?" Dad always asks me about friends. I overheard him and Mum talking once and he said it was weird that I didn't have any "proper mates". I always feel like I am letting Mum and Dad down a bit, by not being "normal" enough.

"Yeah!" I say. "I've got some new mates. Oscar, Max, Blane and Vince. They are all really into football like you and Kai!" I hear him laugh and I feel good, like I'm being the kid he wants me to be. I've never really liked football. I went to a match once with Dad and Kai, but it was too loud and busy and it made my brain get so fizzy it popped. I never went again. I tried learning some football facts so I could join in with their chats, but they knew I wasn't really into it.

"Who do they support?"

"Two of them are United and two are City. They had their hair spray-painted blue and red."

"Brilliant, Reg, that's brilliant. They sound like good lads."

"Yeah," I lie. "They're really cool. I think secondary school's going to be great, actually." Images from the day flash through my mind of me sitting in the corner of the hall counting my breaths, looking around at everyone doing the quizzes, standing alone in the playground and Blane's hand around my neck. Tears threaten my eyeballs and I swallow hard. Nothing is going to plan. It was horrible and I have no chance of making any friends but I can't tell Dad that. I need to fix it before he gets back. To make this lie the truth. I should be able to do it. After all, Michael Gareth hypnotized me into making true friends, didn't he? I just need to show Blane and the others my skills in September.

"That's brilliant. I always thought you needed a few good lads around you."

"Yeah, me too," I say.

When I end the call, I feel a bit strange. I don't like lying to Dad, but it felt good telling him what he wanted to hear. Now I just need to make it true. Thirty-one days to go.

I spend the rest of the weekend practising all of my techniques. I feel like at one point I almost manage to hypnotize myself in the mirror but then I look at the clock and it's one o'clock in the morning, so I think maybe I'm tired and not hypnotized at all.

On Monday morning I can't wait to try it all out on some real human volunteers. At eight o'clock when the Squealers arrive, I'm ready with a plan.

DO TRY THIS AT HOME!

HYPNOTIZE YOUR WAY
TO HAPPINESS

Find a volunteer and ask them to sit
in a chair. Tell them to hold out their
hand in front of them and keep focused
on the back of their hand. Now gently
tap your finger under their wrist, then
on one side, then on the top, and then
on the other side. Repeat this again
and again until you start to feel like
they are zoning out.

When you stop tapping, tell them
to slowly lower their arm and, as
they do, to close their eyes. When
their eyes are closed, you can tell
them that they are in a deep state
of hypnosis. (You can tell when their
eyes are closed but flickering.) Tell
them that when they wake up, they
will desperately want to take you to

the trampoline park, or an ice-cream parlour or to see the monkeys in the zoo. Whatever you end up doing, enjoy!

CHAPTER TWELVE

DO NOT PUT YOUR FINGER INSIDE THE TRAMPOLINE SPRINGS AGAIN

It will get stuck and Mum won't be able to get you out by spreading margarine all over the place. She said next time she would call the fire brigade which would be a bit cool but a lot embarrassing.

Three pairs of eyes are fixed on me as we gently bounce up and down on our bums. I told Mum I would take the Squealers on the trampoline as I know that there is no way she will do it. Last time Mum bounced on the trampoline she ended up peeing her pants. We all found it hysterical, but she didn't seem to find it so funny and has not ventured on for a bounce ever since.

"If you look into my eyes and listen to the sound of my voice you will start to feel sleepy."

"I'm not sleepy, I'm wide awake," squeals Bea. I put my finger to my lips and slowly blink my eyes. I think the gentle movement of the trampoline is helping, as I can see Una and Mabel swaying and staring ahead. I put my hand up to their foreheads and tap between their eyebrows. When I do, Una's eyes close and I know that I've done it.

"Una, when you open your eyes and you hear the sound of the doorbell, you will be the cat that you have always wanted to be. You will purr and meow and stretch like a cat. With every breath you will go deeper and deeper and become more and more like a cat. When the doorbell sounds the cat will come out." I look at Bea who is smiling but not giggling or squealing. She looks relaxed. Mabel's eyes are almost closed.

"Mabel, listen to the sound of my voice. Allow its sound to wash over you, and relax." I tap her forehead again and her eyes gently close. "In a minute I will ask you to open your eyes and when you do, if anyone says your name, you will dance. You will leap and spin and show the world your moves at the very moment you hear your name." I think it's working but every now and then I see one of them open an eye or scratch their nose and I wonder if they are just playing along, thinking it's all just a game.

From what I have read, hypnosis is kind of playing along. It's finding people who will play along, who have minds that are open enough to go along with an idea and allow things to be suggested and just do them. So, even if they are playing along, I guess it's still kind of working. I look at Bea, who is still wide-eyed. I place my hand on her forehead and she blinks her eyes closed. "Bea, you will no longer squeal, your voice will be low and deep. If anyone asks why you are talking that way, you will sing in a low strong voice and call yourself the Beast." I don't think this is going to work but it's worth trying. I carry on. "You are the Beast, you have a deep, deep voice. You are not Bea, and you no longer have any need to squeal. Now all of you just enjoy this feeling of relaxation and as I count back from five, relax even more until I get to one and your eyes will slowly open. Five, four, three, two, one."

As their eyes blink in the sunlight, I look at them and smile, not knowing if it has worked. I'm almost too scared to test it out. I look at Bea and wonder if her voice will be high or low. I almost say Mabel's name to see if she dances but just as I'm about to, Mum's voice calls out over the garden. "Guys, come in for some milk and a snack." The girls all jump up and head off the trampoline, expertly lowering their little bodies on to the grass and then running into the house, leaving me alone to wonder what has just happened. Am I a hypnotist or did they all just close their eyes to make me feel better?

I jump off the trampoline and head to the kitchen. As I approach the open door, I hear Mum's voice, "Bea, you are a funny sausage!" I stop and listen in to see what's happening.

"My name's not Bea," says a very strange, growling voice. "I'm the Beast." My eyes widen and I lean around the door to get a better look. Mum looks slightly confused but she smiles and hands out some crackers.

"Mabel, do you want one, sweetie?" Mabel, at the sound of her name, takes a cracker and spins and dances around the kitchen. I smile. I've done it! Mabel and Bea are hypnotized. Now I just need to test it out on Una.

I raise my hand and press the doorbell and then

peer in to see her reaction. She immediately drops to the floor on all fours and rubs her head against Mum's legs. Mum looks down, wondering what is going on and makes her way to the door.

When she finds me standing there with a daft grin on my face, she narrows her eyes. I can't actually believe this is happening. I have done it. I've really done it. This is it. My life will change now. I can go to school in September and everyone will love me. I can spray-paint my hair and wrestle with Max and Vince. I can make everyone laugh by turning people into chickens. People will look at me the way they looked at Michael Gareth. I will be a hero.

Bea calls through in a deep, gravelly voice, "Who's at the door?" Mabel whooshes past us, leaping into the air and Una meows. Mum looks at me.

"Reggie Houser, what have you done?"

When Mum finally gets the Squealers to stop dancing, meowing and growling by putting their favourite film on, she grabs my arm and pulls me to one side and then hisses under her breath, "Reggie, what did you do to them?"

"Nothing! We were just playing on the trampoline and I was trying out my hypnosis."

"You turned Una into a cat?"

"Only when the doorbell rings," I say, hoping that will make it better.

"Right, well, go and unhypnotize them now, please! I can't have their parents picking them up like this, can I?"

I feel the buzz of my watch reminding me that it's time to let Barnaby out.

"I will do it when I get back from Barnaby's," I say, dashing out of the door and grabbing one of my hypnosis books on the way.

On my way down the street, panic starts to set in. What I didn't mention to Mum was that I have not learnt how to "unhypnotize" someone yet. I have been so focused on the hypnotizing bit, I've kind of skipped all the other bits. I'm pretty sure it will just wear off. I remember listening to one person saying that the effects won't last forever, but I think that was in the chapter about phobias, so I don't know if it counts for turning three-year-olds into dancing, growling cats.

As I let myself into Barnaby's house, he bounds over and licks my face as usual. His leaps and jumps still seem a little bit higher than before he became a frog. Maybe it doesn't just wear off after all.

In the kitchen I see a note on the table next to his treats:

Hi Reggie,

Hope you had a great weekend.

Barnaby has been behaving a bit strangely. We are wondering whether we should take him to the vet as he is off his food and seems to only want to eat worms and flies. He is such a handful anyway, but now we are really worried about him. We think it may be a reaction to the baby.

See how he is and give me a call if there are any problems.

XX

Oh no! Barnaby is still a frog! This is not a good sign for the Squealers. I need to figure out how to reverse it quickly. I let Barnaby into the garden and try and find the right chapter.

Just as I find the bit I need, a text comes through from Mum.

> Reggie, I need you back here now. Una
> just tried to scratch the postman.

I switch my phone off and speed-read the chapter. It turns out that, in all of my listening to audiobooks and reading and researching, I've learned more than I realize. All I need to do to reverse the effects is to tell them it's over. That they no longer want to be a frog or a cat or a dancer. To just let them know that everything is back to normal and they can carry on their lives feeling happy and confident.

I look at Barnaby.

"Right, froggo, time to become a dog again."

As Barnaby is lying down with my finger on his forehead. I decide not just to bring him out of his frog-like trance. I decide to make Barnaby an even better version of himself.

"When you wake up, Barnaby, you will be all dog again, but this time you won't jump on strangers. You will sit at my feet when I ask you. You will fetch a ball instead of chewing it and you will ask politely to get up on the sofa for a belly rub. You will be happy and calm and the best furry big brother to your baby sister. When I stroke your head, you will wake up and be the best version of yourself. Three, two, one."

Barnaby looks at me and yawns and then puts his head on my lap. It's worked. I know it has. He is definitely a dog again. Now on to the Squealers.

*

I've not seen Mum this cross with me since I tried to make an ice rink in the bathroom by mixing flour and water all over the floor and skidding around it in my socks.

"OK, so I don't know how you did it, but you can undo it now, please."

"It's fine, Mum. I know what I'm doing. I just unhypnotized Barnaby so I know it will work."

"You hypnotized the dog too? Reggie! What did you do to him?"

"He thought he was a frog."

"That's not possible, Reggie. Dogs don't know what frogs are, so how could he become one?"

"Well, he was hopping a lot and eating flies," I say, considering what Mum has just said. How would Barnaby know how to act like a frog? Maybe she's right.

"You said that dog was a bit loopy anyway, you probably just sent him loopier."

"Well, whatever, he's OK now. I fixed it, so I will fix the Squealers too." Then remembering the bonuses that I added on to Barnaby. "Can I make them a bit less squealy though?"

"No, Reggie. Make them exactly the same as they were before. Then we need to have a serious conversation about this hypnosis malarky."

*

Back on the trampoline, the Squealers have opened their eyes and are blinking in the normality.

Una looks a bit sad. "I liked being a cat," she says. "I think I might stay as a cat."

"That's fine," I say. "Just not this afternoon, if that's OK? Mum needs to know that you are not a cat for now." She sticks out her bottom lip and hisses at me.

"Let's bounce!" squeals Bea in the highest pitch I have ever heard. "Bounce, Mabel, bounce!" Mabel doesn't dance and I sit at the edge and watch as they bounce and squeal. Squeal and bounce. I smile to myself. Mum might be right, Barnaby couldn't possibly know how to behave like a frog, but I definitely hypnotized him into being weird and I hypnotized the girls. I can do it. I know I can do it.

I look at my calendar and draw a picture of a cat with swirly eyes on today's square. I have twenty-nine days left to practise before school starts. There is no way Mum is going to let me try it again on the Squealers. The dog is too doggy. Who else is there to practise on?

After the Squealers have gone, Mum makes herself a cup of tea and sits down at the table. She looks very serious, and I know that I'm in trouble.

"Reggie, I don't know what happened today. I don't know if any of it was real but what you are messing around with, controlling people's minds and making people do things, it's dangerous."

"Making someone dance or meow isn't dangerous!" I laugh.

"Making anyone do anything that they are not in control of is incredibly dangerous, Reggie. We always have to choose our reactions to things and know our own minds."

"That's what Michael Gareth said. Know your own mind. But I'm figuring out everyone else's mind, Mum. Don't you think it's amazing?"

"I don't want you messing about with this stuff any more, Reggie."

"But I love it and it makes me feel good, Mum. When I'm talking in my hypnotist voice and saying calm things, I feel different to normal. My brain gets less buzzy. And I think I might actually be really good at it. It's going to change my life. I'm actually going to make friends."

"And that's wonderful, but you can't go round turning people into things, making them do stuff against their will."

"You can only hypnotize people who want to be hypnotized, Mum. People whose minds are open. The Squealers loved it. Una wants to be a cat!"

"No, Reggie, listen to me. I want you to stop it."

"But—"

"NO!"

I feel so confused. I have finally found something I am good at. Something that will get me some friends and make me happy and Mum says it's dangerous. She didn't say that when Michael Gareth was doing it. She didn't say that when she thought I would never be able to do it so why now? Why, when I am just starting to figure it out? My head hurts and I don't want to look at her serious face any more. She has made me cross and confused and like I don't know anything. But I do know something, I know I want to be a hypnotist. I know my own mind and so I don't care what she says. I will just have to carry on in secret.

DO TRY THIS AT HOME!

SELF-HYPNOSIS

This one takes some time. Find a quiet spot and get comfy. Turn off all your beeps and buzzes and leave your phone, iPad and any other distracting gadgets somewhere else. Find a spot on the wall opposite you. A smudge or a nail or the join between the wall and ceiling; anything to focus on. Now, as you look at the spot, tell yourself that with each breath, your eyelids will get heavy. Do this until you can't stop them from closing.

When they are closed, imagine walking down ten steps. At the bottom is a door; go through the door into a wonderful garden. Take a seat or lie on the grass and relax. Now imagine that one of your arms is getting heavier and heavier. As you feel one of your arms weighing more and more you will know that you are in a hypnotic state. If you are really good, you won't even be able to lift the heavy arm if you try!

Now you can tell yourself whatever you want. Do you want to try harder at school? Do you want to run faster or be less shy? Tell yourself that you will be able to achieve whatever you want and then when you are ready, walk back up those stairs and wake yourself up slowly. You should feel happy, relaxed and confident. (Or you may have fallen asleep and be snoring and dribbling.)

CHAPTER THIRTEEN

FIRST DAY OF SCHOOL

Do not tell any of your long stories. When you meet the spray-hair gang, play it cool. Mum says that even though she loves your stories, other people find them hard to follow. Just nod and listen and laugh along, then you can hit them with some mind control.

With no one other than myself to practise on, by the time the first day of school comes around I have mastered self-hypnosis. I'm sleeping better than ever, as I can switch my brain off in a way I never could before. I have learned so many different ways to hypnotize people, I can't wait to try them out. Mum thinks I've given up. I told her that I'm now really into the idea of becoming a dog trainer. She thinks I've been listening to dog-training audiobooks and I spent most of my time round at Barnaby's practising my skills.

Barnaby is now the perfect dog and his owners can't quite believe what has happened. On the last day of the holidays, when Dan was paying me, he looked at Barnaby sitting perfectly at his feet while Lulu gurgled in her carrier.

"Reggie, I honestly don't know how to thank you. I'll be honest, I'm terrified that without you coming over every day, he'll go back to his old ways!"

I smile. It feels good having done something useful. For someone to find me helpful rather than annoying. "He will be fine," I say. "If you need me to help after school or at the weekends, just let me know."

"Definitely. If you don't mind, I have been telling other dog owners at the park all about you. They couldn't believe the change in Barnaby either. You may have found yourself a good little job."

I smile and give Lulu's cheek a squeeze as I leave.

It feels weird that the summer is over. I feel like a

different kid to the one I was at the end of primary school. I'm embarrassed when I think about rolling down the hill and running home with my arms out like an aeroplane. Even though secretly I wish I could roll down hills forever, at least now I have something new. I wish I had known how to hypnotize myself at primary school. Maybe then I wouldn't have got into so much trouble. Maybe I would have had some friends.

As I walk towards school on the first day, my heart is beating fast and my face is tingling. I can't stop rubbing my hands together and the energy in my body feels fizzier and buzzier than it has for ages. I stop walking and try counting up and down from three and closing my eyes every time I get to one, but I still feel too awake. I try to roll my eyes back until they flicker but all I can hear is the sound of kids, everywhere. It's very different doing all of my tricks, inductions and skills when I am surrounded by noise and busyness.

I have pictured this day a thousand different ways. The best of them all is the whole school surrounding me as I hypnotize the gang. Everyone laughing and saying how cool I am. Then Blane and Max and the others pulling me towards them in a wrestly type hug and telling me that I'm one of them and they will look after me no matter what. The worst first day I have imagined I am trying to blank out of my mind, but thoughts about my hypnosis not working and tight hands around my neck keep popping back into my head. With each thought a new wave of either excitement or fear spreads through me.

I feel a hard slap on my back and turn to see one of the older boys – Blane, I think – standing behind me. His hair is now back to its normal mousey colour.

"Got some first-day nerves, kid?"

"Kind of," I say.

"There's nothing to worry about," he says, smiling as Max joins him and adds:

"Apart from us, that is."

I smile awkwardly as if they are joking, even though I know they are not.

"I've been looking forward to seeing you hypnotize Max here," Blane says. "That's if you can still do it?"

I nod my head, hoping that I can.

"Meet us at the bike park at lunch."

"OK," I say, feeling scared but also pleased that he has spoken to me. This will be my chance to make the best version of my day actually come true.

In my form class I don't recognize anyone, apart

from Vince. He has normal-coloured hair now. I smile and give him a half wave but he's too busy throwing a bottle and trying to make it land on the table. There are groups of kids who look like they know each other, and I go and stand next to one of them and lean on the table and listen to their conversation as if I'm part of it. One of the boys gives me a funny look but no one tells me to move. They are talking about some YouTuber I have never heard of, so I keep my mouth shut and stop myself from jiggling by squeezing one hand down hard on to the other.

When the bell goes, they all sit down and find someone to sit with. I head towards Vince but he sits next to a boy who looks twice as old as me. Everyone finds a seat until there is just me left and no more spaces. I look around the room and try and find somewhere close to the boys that I was just with but there is nothing. The whole class seems to have found someone apart from me. Then the teacher comes in.

"Good morning, everyone." She has small glasses on a string around her neck and a beaky-looking face. "Sit down, please," she says, looking at me.

I look around again not knowing where to go.

"There is a space here at the front."

I look to where she is pointing. A tiny girl with

hair that looks like a ponytail full of bubbles and bobbles turns to look at me and smiles a huge smile. She has big braces on her teeth. There is something familiar about her, but I think it's just because she is smiling at me as if she knows me. I don't really want to sit with her but as I'm pausing and looking around, the teacher snaps, "Now, please!" So I shuffle to the front and slide into the chair.

"I'm Lily. Lily Stevenson," says the tiny girl, still with a huge grin on her face. I just nod. "What's your name?" she whispers.

"Reggie."

"SHHHH!" comes the voice of the teacher who is scowling at me. How have I managed to get into trouble already, when I have not even done anything?

I get through the morning without my maths or science teachers telling me off. I do end up having to sit next to Lily for the whole morning though. She follows me to each classroom and plonks herself next to me as if we have made some plan. It's like she thinks we are best friends or something. In science I get up to move away from her but her face looks sad, and when I turn around all the lads are already sitting with each other so I sit down again, which puts the daft grin back on Lily's face.

When the bell for lunch goes, I smile and take a breath. Here goes – my chance to show people my skills and find a proper gang of my own.

"Not everyone can be hypnotized," I say as they all gather around me. I'm feeling weirdly calm now that I'm actually about to hypnotize them. Like this is my house and they are coming into it. That's how hypnosis has started making me feel, like I am in control for a change. Even when I'm just doing it to myself in the mirror. It's a nice feeling. I think it's what those kids must feel like who are really great at tests or at sport. Maybe that's just what confidence feels like and I've never really felt it before.

I haven't seen Oscar all morning. He's in the other half of the year and now that his hair is a normal colour, it was not easy to spot him in assembly. He's here now, standing behind the other three.

"Here we go," says Blane. "Excuses, excuses."

"It's true," I say. "I can try and hypnotize you all and it might work on one of you. That's better than me just trying it on Max."

"What will you make us do though?" says Oscar, looking worried. Oscar seems a bit different from the others. Quieter.

"What do you want me to make you do?" I ask, smiling.

"It's not going to work anyway," Max says. "Just let him do it."

I tell them to sit on the wall by the bikes and to focus on the lamp post in the distance. Then I count and ask them to close their eyes. At first they are giggling and nudging each other but after a while they are still and their eyes are opening and closing like they should be. When I suggest that their eyes become heavy and won't open, I instantly see that Blane is awake and maybe Oscar too. I keep going, and even though I don't think it's working on them, they stay quiet and watch the other two.

"The more you try to open your eyes, the deeper you go into hypnosis and the heavier your eyelids become." I keep looking at their closed eyes and see the flickering of Max's eyes beneath his lids, a sure sign that it's working.

"OK, so when you try to open your eyes, the harder you try, the deeper you go and the more they will not open." One of Vince's eyes flicks open, leaving Max clearly trying and failing to open his eyes. Now I need to think of something to make him do. Something that will prove my skills and make the others laugh and want to be my friend. Even though they are still a bit scary, I know that if they were my friends they would look out for me. They are a proper gang and that's what I want. That's what I have been practising for all summer. I take a breath in, knowing that this is a big moment.

"When I count to three, Max, you will open your eyes and whenever anyone says the name Reggie you will shout, 'Reggie is the king!' at the top of your voice." Then I repeat myself just to make sure the suggestion has landed.

As I count to three, I see the others all trying desperately not to laugh and holding on to each other. They know as well as I do that it's working. I'm impressing them, I just know it.

"… three. OK, Max, open your eyes." He blinks and looks around.

"Who is Reggie?"

Max looks up and shouts, "Reggie is the king!"

The others fall about laughing. Then they all start saying my name and howling with laughter every time Max shouts the words. After a while I see Max smiling too and I think it is starting to wear off. I wonder if he is playing along now but it doesn't matter. It worked. They are having fun. I really made them laugh.

"Right, Max, when I count to three and click my fingers, you will be wide awake and you will feel happy and full of energy." I count and click and Max shakes his head, laughing. "That was weird, bruv," he says.

"Were you just messing though?" asks Blane.

"Kind of. I knew what I was doing, but I kind of wanted to do it and almost couldn't help myself."

"Those are some mad skills you've got, Reggie."

"Thanks," I say, still smiling.

"I reckon we could make some decent money out of this, don't you, boys?" They look at each other and nod their heads as if they are all thinking the same thing.

"Reggie, you are one of us now, kid." Blane puts his arm around me and grips my shoulder tightly. I can't help but grin a huge, cheesy grin. It's worked!

"Do you want to make some money, Reggie?" My eyes widen and I nod. "We love making money, don't we, lads?"

DO TRY THIS AT HOME!

MATHS

This one feels like one of those
horrible maths questions where they
ask you to do maths but are also
talking about Lucy buying apples and
giving them to Peter. Stick with it
though, because it's a good one when
it works. Ask your volunteer (someone
old enough and bright enough to do
some pretty simple maths) to think
of a number between 1 and 10. Tell
them to multiply it by 9. If it has two
digits tell them to add the two digits
together. They have to do all of this
in their heads without telling you or
counting on their fingers or out loud.
Now they take away 5. Then they turn
the number in their head into a letter
by going through the alphabet until
they get to their number. I.e. 1=a, 2=b,

3=c etc. Then ask them to think of a country beginning with that letter. Then using the second letter of the country, think of an animal – the first animal that pops into their head. What is the colour of the animal? Then say "But they don't have grey elephants in Denmark". If you get it right it's so worth all of the maths!

CHAPTER FOURTEEN

PENCIL CASE!!!

If you take your pencil case out of your bag to draw fake glasses on yourself in felt tip, remember to put it back in afterwards. If you forget to take it to school again you will get a negative and Mum will be cross.

I spend the next few days searching for the gang. I go to the bike park every lunch but they aren't there. In science I ask Vince where they hang out and he just taps his nose and says, "Blane will find you. We've got plans for you, Reggie boy." I feel relieved that they haven't forgotten about me.

They scare me but I still want to be part of their

group. They are different to everyone else. They don't look scared. I want some of that for myself. The other kids in my class, even the boys who all chat and look like they will become the popular gang, look young and wary. Now that I'm friends with Blane and his gang I won't be scared of anything any more. It is almost like they are hypnotizing me towards them and I can't stop it.

I hang around in the playground hoping that they will grab me and tell me their money-making plan, but I don't see them anywhere. As each day passes and I'm on my own, wandering down the halls or sitting on the grass by the football pitches, I think that I would do anything the gang asked me to do. Anything that would make me feel less alone.

The only time that I'm not alone is when Lily finds me. She is following me around now between lessons, as well as sitting next to me. I don't know why. She says that she gets lost easily and follows me between the classrooms, but the way she stares and smiles at me makes me nervous. No one in the class wants to talk to her. I heard Esme and Amna, the two most popular girls in the class, talking about her. They think she is weird and babyish. I kind of feel sorry for her because maybe I'm a bit the same, but I don't really want to be her friend, even though she lent me a pen yesterday and totally saved me from Mr "Angry" Andrews. Two weirdos together make it even less likely that people will want to be friends with us. I want a group of lads like Kai and Dad have. I don't want some feeble little girl with weird hairstyles.

Every day her hair is more and more strange. Different plaits all winding around her head and puffs of hair poking out of the top. Today there is a heart shape made out of hair on the back of her head. I have no idea how she does it and I can't stop staring at it.

"My sister is training to be a hairdresser," she whispers in maths as she sees me looking at the back of her head. "It's beautiful, isn't it?"

I ignore her and look at my book. She's always smiling and constantly asks if I need help and wants to work on questions together. I just want her to leave me alone, and for there to be a space next to Vince so I can move seats.

When my head gets fuzzy or I can't sit still, I quietly hypnotize myself. Silently scanning through my body and relaxing each muscle or tapping my finger on my wrist. I catch a couple of the kids whispering and laughing as they watch me so I try to do it in a way that's not too obvious. It doesn't always work and sometimes if I don't catch my busy brain in time, I have to ask to go to the toilet so that I can get out of the classroom and run down the corridor.

I manage not to shout out too much or get into too much trouble for the first few days, but when I put my hand up to answer a question in history I completely forget what I am meant to be saying. I end up telling the whole class a story about my dad having a poo drop on his back when he was pipe fitting once. They all laugh hysterically but the teacher looks a bit disgusted and annoyed. Sometimes my stories start in one place and end up somewhere completely different and no one, including me, quite knows how I got there. The teacher doesn't tell me off though, he just brings it back to the Tudors and carries on. I feel like because they all laughed, some of the boys might think I'm funny and want to hang out with me. Maybe I could hypnotize them and make them all like me. But when I try and sit with them at lunch they tell me the seats are taken and then I hear one of them calling me "Poo Back" and giggling, so I don't think it's worked after all. I need to stay focused on Oscar, Vince, Blane and Max; they are the lads for me.

Mum is so happy with me. She says that she feels like I "have turned a corner". Because I didn't get into trouble in the summer holidays and now have managed a few days at school without a phone call home she thinks I'm some wonder child. It's so hard not to tell her that it's all because I ignored her and carried on learning mind control, but somehow I manage to keep it in.

I've never really had a secret from Mum, apart from the time I caught a mouse and tried to keep it as a pet in a shoebox under my bed. That secret didn't end so well. The mouse bit me and I screamed and had to go to the doctor's for an injection. Mum was really angry. I don't want to keep it secret, and it feels bad, but I know that I need to do this. It's important.

Today at lunch the gang finally find me eating my chips and beans. Lily is obviously sitting next to me, as always.

"Who's your girlfriend?" Blane says with a snort. I laugh along but Lily narrows her eyes and huffs at him. "Right, Reggie boy, let's help you with your dinner, and then we can show you the plan." They all grab a handful of chips until my plate is empty, and shove them in their mouths. I smile, not even caring that my tummy is rumbling. They are talking to me. They came to find me and they have a plan that includes me. This is it, everything that I wanted to happen is happening.

"Meet us by the bike park in five minutes," Blane says.

"You're gonna love this," adds Oscar. Then they all leave and I see the teacher on the door shake her head as they pass.

I've seen Blane sitting outside the head teacher's office twice already this week. When I go for my toilet breaks I always sneak past to see who is in trouble. Oscar was there on Tuesday. When he saw me, he said, "What are you doing here? Have they sent you out too?"

"No," I say. "I'm just having a wander. What did you do?"

"I didn't know any of the answers so I didn't do any of the work. He thought I was being naughty, but I just didn't know what he was on about." He sighed and looked really sad. I didn't know what else to say so I carried on walking. Whenever I saw Blane there, I hid. He scares me the most out of all of them.

As I stack my tray to leave, Lily looks at me seriously and says, "I don't think you should go, Reggie." Then she takes a sip of her drink and adds,

"I don't think they are kind people, and my mum says you should only surround yourself with kindness."

"Shut up, Lily. You don't know anything about them. They're my mates."

"They didn't seem like mates to me. Mates don't steal your chips and mates aren't mean." A memory flicks back into my head of Michael Gareth asking me what makes a good friend. I shake it off and frown, turning on Lily.

"Well, what would you know? You're not my mate either, so stop following me around, OK?" She looks sad and like she might cry, which makes me feel bad, but I shove it down and carry on loading my tray.

"I knew this was a bad idea. I just want to be your friend," she mumbles as she sniffs into a tissue.

"Just leave me alone, Lily. I don't want to be your friend. I don't even know you. I've got mates, OK?" I say quietly.

I leave the dinner hall and head towards the doors and out to the bike park, where the gang will be waiting for me.

As I approach the shed, I see Vince holding a sign:

GET HIPNOTYZEd FOR A POUNd!!!!!

I smile. This could be perfect. Everyone will get to know me and find out that I'm part of this gang at the same time. And we will make some money!

"You've spelt it wrong," I say. Vince looks angrily at the others.

"I told you it was wrong," he says. "I haven't got any more paper."

Blane takes the sign and screws it up. He pats me on the shoulder.

"So, Reggie, this is the plan."

They tell me that every lunchtime I will come here and hypnotize whoever turns up. They've found a chair from somewhere, and Oscar says he is going to bring in his mum's old curtains to hang up to make it look like a little booth. They all seem so excited and must have been talking about it a lot.

"We'll make loads of money! Everyone will want a go."

I look at their faces and the empty chair and shrug my shoulders. "All right," I say. "It'll be fun."

Blane shakes my hand and it makes me feel really special. I can't keep the grin off my face. Then he bends down so that we're the same height.

"Now the thing is, we need to advertise your skills.

No one is going to want you to hypnotize them if they don't believe you can do it."

"So, what will you do?" I ask, thinking that they'll make flyers or put it on Instagram or something.

"It's not what *we* will do, Reggie, it's what *you* will do." Blane smiles, and I get a shiver down my spine. "Tomorrow, in assembly, you'll hypnotize Mr Gray. Then everyone will know how good you are. You'll be a hero, Reggie. The best thing that has ever happened in school. You'll go down in history."

"I can't hypnotize the head teacher!" I say.

"Yes, you can, Reggie. You can hypnotize the head teacher."

"But I'll get into so much trouble! My mum told me I had to stop doing it."

Blane looks at the others and they all close in.

"You will be a legend, Reggie."

"And you will get to hang out with us every lunch."

"This is the most important part of the plan, Reggie."

I look at their faces and I want to make them happy. If I say no then they might ditch me.

"OK, I'll do it."

DO TRY THIS AT HOME!

THE FINGER TRICK

Find a volunteer. (It has to be a human volunteer. You can't do this mind trick with a dog, teddy bear or a block of cheese, however much they want to try it.) Ask the human to put their hands together and interlock their fingers and clasp them. Then ask them to raise their index fingers (if your volunteer is a ninny and has no clue of the difference between their thumbs and their pinkies, you can show them that the index fingers are the ones next to their thumbs). Their two index fingers should be up in the air and apart with the other fingers still interlocked. There should be a gap the size of about three Maltesers between their index fingers. You will now control their minds and make their fingers come together without touching them. Holding your finger above theirs and pointing it down, make circles around their raised fingers. Keep going until their fingers come together, as if you are tying them up with an imaginary thread. Take a bow and, as they gasp and cheer and shout, "More!", enjoy the smug feeling of controlling someone's mind — and fingers!

CHAPTER FIFTEEN

TOP TEN THINGS THAT GET ME INTO TROUBLE:

1. Shouting out

2. Throwing my pencil case in the air

3. Farting

4. Singing a song

5. Jiggling

6. Yawning loudly

7. Burping

8. Drawing on myself

9. Standing up

10. Telling the truth

Obviously I can't just hypnotize Mr Gray from my seat in the hall. I'm good but not that good. When I tell the gang this, Blane gets really angry and tells me that I just need to figure it out. He says that if Mr Gray doesn't turn into a chicken one way or another in tomorrow's assembly, I'm dead. Then he storms off. Max says that Blane is just stressed because he's so excited about the plan and wants me to become a legend. Oscar and Vince nod along and just say that I can do it and they totally believe in me. Then they follow Blane and leave me alone in my hypnosis chair by the bike park.

My brain is darting about, wondering what I should do. This feels really bad and scary, but the idea of becoming a school hero is also exciting and makes me feel buzzy in a good way. I definitely don't want to make Blane angry, that's for sure. I've got to do this.

Just as I'm thinking about how on earth I can get close enough to Mr Gray before tomorrow morning, the bell goes and an idea pops into my head. I stand up, grab my bag and head back towards school, knowing exactly what I need to do.

The first lesson in the afternoon is geography with Mr Dunn. It's so boring. He talks in the slowest voice and shows us really dull pictures of rivers. As I listen to him drone on and look around the room at the glazed expressions on everyone's faces, I think Mr Dunn would probably make a very good hypnotist. Lily is sitting next to me, twiddling with her hair, still looking sad, and I know that now is the time. I have to do something. Something bad enough to get sent to Mr Gray, but hopefully not bad enough that he will ring my mum. I remember all the things I did in primary that got me in trouble and go through them, checking them off in my head and thinking of reasons why they won't work.

Then I think of the one. The thing that I need to do. The thing that will definitely get me kicked out. The thing that will not make the rest of the class think I'm weird. The thing that I actually want to do anyway. As soon as I have thought it, it happens. Like it's out of my control and I couldn't stop it if I tried. I stand up and the words come clearly out of my mouth.

"Sir, this is the most boring lesson I've ever been in."

Lily turns to me. "Reggie, no, stop it!" I ignore her and look defiantly back at Mr Dunn.

It works. His face goes red and I feel instantly bad, but then everyone giggles and the laughs make me feel a bit better. It takes him a moment to find the words and then, still in his dull tone, he says, "Please leave the classroom and go and see Mr Gray immediately."

On my way to Mr Gray's office I stop in the corridor. My brain is really fizzing and everything in my body is tingling. Thoughts about Mum, Lily, the gang and assembly all compete for attention and I can't get rid of them. I need to clear my head before I see Mr Gray. I need to hypnotize myself and tell myself it's all going to be OK, before I can try and hypnotize him. I stop and close my eyes.

"Why have you been sent out?" Mr Gray says, in a way that makes me think he has asked this question a thousand times already today. I look into his eyes and slowly move my gaze and his eyes follow. "What's your name?" he asks, but I raise my finger, sway it for a few seconds and before he can ask again I click.

His head lolls forward on to his chest. I've just hypnotized the head teacher! I get up and pump my fist into the air silently. I smile, breathe in and sit back down. Now I just need to make him become a chicken tomorrow morning when I give the signal in the whole school assembly.

"Mr Gray, when you wake up you will feel happy and full of energy and you will send me back to class. When you hear the words 'It's chicken time' you will truly believe you are a chicken and want the whole world to know about it. The words are 'It's chicken time'."

When he wakes up and smiles and sends me back to lessons my heart is thumping through my chest. It feels like the biggest day of my life. Tomorrow is when the entire school find out that I'm a hypnotist and I become a legend.

"Everyone, sit down, please. Quietly!"

We're all filing into the hall and it feels like the room is alive with excitement, even though it's only me and the gang who know what is about to happen.

I'm going to wait until he has started and then give the signal. I've made a plan in case it doesn't work. If I give the signal and he doesn't change, I'm going to run out of the hall and pretend I'm sick. Then I will get sent home, and the gang won't be able to kill me.

As Mr Gray begins a talk about the dangers of social media, my heart starts beating in my chest. I can feel each thud inside my head like a ticking clock counting down to my moment. When I can't cope any more and my brain feels like it's about to explode, I stand up, wave my arms in the air and shout, "It's chicken time!"

There is a pause, and I think that it's not worked. The kids near to me start giggling and whispering, and I know that if this doesn't work, then I'm in trouble. Everyone will think I'm a weirdo, shouting about chickens in the middle of assembly. It HAS to work. I look desperately at Mr Gray. He looks back at me, a little confused, but there is no anger or threat in his expression. So I double down, hoping that he just needs an extra nudge. Another suggestion to send him over the edge.

"It's chicken time!" I call, louder and more confident this time.

Slowly but surely Mr Gray's back starts to hunch, his elbows pop out at the sides and he begins to peck towards the floor. Kids are looking from me to him, gobsmacked. It looks completely bizarre and ridiculous and the whole room starts to shuffle and wriggle. The wriggles turn into giggles when a strange noise emerges from Mr Gray. I'm not sure if it's what I would call a *cluck* but it definitely sounds more chicken-like than human.

The hall slowly realizes what's happening. They have heard what I called out and are now looking at a head chicken strutting around the stage. The noise in the audience builds, getting louder with every peck or cluck. Kids are howling. Everyone starts making chicken noises and the whole room turns into a poultry farm. Flapping elbows and the occasional sound of a *cock-a-doodle-doo*. The kids are more like chickens than Mr Gray; it's as though I have hypnotized the entire hall. I can't help laughing. Seeing what I have created makes me feel so happy. Powerful. I did all of this just using mind control. I feel like I could do anything. This is going better than I ever could have imagined. With a few more lurches and jerks of his head he looks out to the audience, eyes wide, flaps his elbows and runs off the stage.

The school erupts and the noise of laughter, confusion and joy is deafening. People are turning to look at me and start swarming around me, asking questions. Older kids who would never normally talk to me are looking at me like I'm their hero.

"Did you do that?"

"What's your name?"

A couple of the boys in my class who usually

ignore me come over and laugh with me as if they know me.

"Why did you turn him into a chicken?"

"You're awesome, Reggie."

I ignore Lily's confused expression from across the hall. I don't care what she thinks. A slow smile grows on my face, but before I can answer anybody, I feel a strong pat on my shoulder and look up to see Vince on one side and Blane on the other.

"He's our mate," says Vince proudly, and I put my arm around him and grin. I feel so happy.

"If you want to see his skills, bring a quid to the bike park at lunchtime," Blane adds coolly.

Then a teacher who I have never seen before scurries on to the stage and we all sit back in our seats.

"Mr Gray is not feeling well," she says, looking alarmed. "Everyone, make your way to your first lesson." And as the noise erupts once more and everyone re-enacts Mr Gray's chicken moves, I can hear her small voice calling out, "Sensibly, please."

I walk to my next lesson with a spring in my step. Everyone is looking at me and whispering or calling out my name. They all think I'm the best. Blane and the lads were so right: this is exactly what they said would happen. This is what I have wanted forever. To walk through school and not be hated or annoying. It's just like I thought it would be. Instead of feeling like a weirdo and a loner, I'm loved. Everyone knows me now. Vince said I was his mate and people thought I was amazing. I never want this moment to end. This is exactly why I didn't want to give up hypnotism. Mum was so wrong.

At lunchtime, the queue for the hypnosis chair stretches out towards the playground. Oscar and Vince are in charge of organizing it and snaking the line up and down in a way that the teachers won't be able to see from the classroom windows. Max and Blane are at the front taking the money.

By the end of lunch I've tried to hypnotize about thirty kids. Some of them worked and others didn't, but if they complained then Blane threatened to punch them or put them in a headlock and told them to come back tomorrow and try again. No one had any chance of getting a refund. I start to see a pattern for the kids who my tricks work on and the ones where it doesn't.

I have read loads about suggestibility and why some people can't be controlled. The kids who come in with wide eyes and a big, goofy smile and tell me that they think what I did in assembly was the coolest thing ever are the easiest. I barely have to do anything. They are so eager to believe it that I could just click my fingers and say sleep and they would immediately fall on the floor. I wouldn't need to do any tapping or counting or tricks with their eyes.

Some kids come in and think they are above it all. They are here to prove me wrong and think they can explain everything. You can tell by their narrow eyes and serious faces. Only cracking the occasional fake smile. These are kids who would never let me hypnotize them; they would fight against every moment. By the end of lunch, I can spot them and so I don't even try. I just nod to Max and he removes them from the chair and tells them to come back tomorrow.

The quiet ones who don't give anything away and look worried or scared are the interesting ones. These are the kids I want to hypnotize. But I don't want to turn them into animals or make them fall asleep every time anyone says their name. These kids I want to help. I want to make them braver or louder. I want to send them back into their lessons being able to put their hand up and read out in front of the class. I want to give them the courage to ask someone if they want to sit with them or hang out at lunch.

When a quiet boy called Freddie from my class sits in the chair, I ask him to close his eyes and when I have him relaxed and open I start.

"Freddie, I want you to imagine the doors of the school. Every time you walk through those doors you are going to feel bigger, stronger and happier than you have ever felt before."

Blane frowns and interrupts, which will probably ruin the hypnosis.

"Stick with the funny stuff, Reggie. That's what will keep 'em coming back."

I think about it and risk whispering back, "Don't you think if we have a school full of animals the teachers will clock that something is happening? If I mix it up, they may take longer to find us."

He looks angry and confused at first and then Max whispers something in his ear.

"Yeah, all right. Do other stuff too. But make sure some of it is funny, all right?"

I nod my head and carry on making Freddie feel like the best version of himself. Blane and Max listened to me. They know that I am good at this. It feels amazing to have everything I want all at the same time. To have my new friends around me, helping me to use my hypnotism for good. I can feel that I am making everyone happier, whether it's making them laugh at something silly or doing something important. This is exactly where I am supposed to be. I smile as the next kid looks up at me from the chair with large, hopeful eyes. This one will be easy, I think to myself. I think this one might have to be a pig.

DO TRY THIS AT HOME!

FEELING LUCKY?

This is a good one to do with your class at school. You can impress someone in particular with it. Tell the class that you are going to predict who is the luckiest person in the room. Tell everyone to shout out their names and you will pretend to write them on pieces of paper. Actually, you will only write the name of the "chosen one" every time you are writing, but do it in a way that no one can see. Fold each piece up and put it into a hat, or if there are not many kids at your school who wear top hats then find something else. When all the names are in, tell everyone to look at you. You will now sense from their eyes who is the luckiest. Write the chosen one's name large on a board

or piece of paper and show the room.
Now choose a different volunteer and
pretend to control their mind. Place
the hat (or whatever) on top of their
heads so they can't see inside and ask
them to choose a piece of paper. When
they open the paper and reveal the
matching name you will be a hero.

CHAPTER SIXTEEN

**When you are getting told off, try to stop
wriggling. If it's Mum, then look at her
fringe so she thinks you are listening. If she
thinks you are not looking at her, it goes on
for longer and is way worse.**

When I get home from school, Mum is out with the
Squealers and so I run upstairs to my room with a
bag of crisps and start making a plan for all the kids
I can't hypnotize. What I'm realizing is that people
just want to believe in something. Something magical
or something inexplicable that makes them gasp
or laugh or both. In all of the books I've read and
listened to and all of the websites I've been on, there
is a mixture of hypnosis, magic and suggestion, so

maybe for the kids who won't go under, I need to just show them a trick. Read their mind, or dazzle them with my memory. Something that makes it worth them giving their precious pound.

After lunch Blane and Max counted up the money and gave me a fiver. I don't know how many kids sat in the chair today, but I know they will have got a lot more than a fiver. When they walked away I heard them talking about how much they were going to make. I felt a bit weird about it for a second, but without them I wouldn't be doing any of this so maybe it's OK. Anyway, school was the best it's ever been. I'm a hero, I have a new gang and I am making money. It's like all my dreams are coming true. After lunch everyone was arguing over who would sit next to me. I ended up with Vince obviously and I didn't mind when he got us into trouble by throwing pens at Lucy Davis, or when he drew a moustache on us both with a Sharpie. I ignored Lily's sad face as she sat on her own with all of her things laid out neatly in front of her.

We got the giggles so bad when Harry Fooge, one of my most suggestible lunchtime clients, shouted "Mummy" when the bell went. I pictured all the other classrooms full of hypnotized kids turning into monkeys or shouting things out. The best thing was seeing Freddie put his hand up and answer a question with a smile on his face. He looked happier than ever. Sitting with Vince and messing about and seeing everything that I had done made me feel so good. I want to keep doing it and I want to impress even the kids that I can't hypnotize.

As I'm deciding on the tricks I will use tomorrow, I hear the door close downstairs.

"Hi, Mum," I call.

I can hear voices so I know that she's not alone, so I carry on jotting down my top five tricks. Then I hear her voice calling upstairs and I know instantly that I have a problem.

"Reggie, come here, please."

I can always tell when I'm in trouble. Her voice goes lower and slower and sounds dangerous. This is not good. I have been so caught up in the day and everything that happened that I haven't even let myself think about being rumbled. Until now. The panic starts filling my brain and making my head hurt. I have no idea how to get out of this.

I reluctantly make my way downstairs and when I get to the kitchen, I see Dad standing at the door. My face breaks into a huge grin.

"Dad!" I shout and run towards him, grabbing him in a tight hug. He hugs me back for a minute, then holds me away from him.

"Reg, you've been lying to your mum."

I look from him to Mum and see their serious faces. My brain goes into panic, not knowing what I should do. Wanting to go straight back into a hug with Dad and ignore the cross look. I close my eyes and pretend it's not really happening.

But Mum speaks and I can't ignore it.

"The school have been on the phone, Reggie."

I look at her and try and make my eyes bigger and more innocent looking. I don't know exactly what she knows. Is this about Mr Gray or the hypno chair? I don't want to give anything away so I just keep my eyes wide.

"It's your first week, Reg. I'm so disappointed."

I hate it when she says she's disappointed. I would rather she were anything than that. Angry, horrified, upset, but disappointed is the worst.

I don't know what to say and my eyes flick around the room, landing on different objects. I can hear the fridge buzzing in the background and it makes me feel fuzzy and distracted. My fingers are wringing together, squeezing hard. I can't find any words and in the silence Mum looks at me and seems to get more upset.

"Look at him, Kevin, he doesn't even listen to me." She looks like she might cry. Dad grabs my arm.

"Look at your mother when she's speaking to you, Reggie. This is not what I wanted to come home to, son. I mean, I know what it's like being a kid. God knows I got into my fair share of trouble, but could you not just get through the first week? Your mum's exhausted."

Then Mum seems to get some more energy.

"You said you would stop with the whole ridiculous hypnosis thing, Reggie. You lied to my face."

"What did they say?" I mumble, trying to keep my eyes on Mum as I speak but still listening to the buzz of the fridge.

"What did they say?!" She practically screams this. "They said you hypnotized the head teacher, Reggie. The HEAD TEACHER! They said that all the poor man remembered was you saying things about chickens. They said that they had never dealt with anything like this in the history of the school. They had to send him home; they thought he was in shock! The poor man hasn't been well anyway."

"I didn't do anything bad, I promise. I didn't make him ill."

"Luckily I managed to convince them that you are rubbish at hypnosis and there is no way you could have turned anyone into a chicken."

"I did though," I say, suddenly feeling defensive.

"No, you didn't, Reggie," Dad says firmly.

"The school are choosing to believe that Mr Gray had a fever and was experiencing hallucinations and convulsions, which would account for his strange behaviour, and I think you would do well to go along with the story, don't you, Reggie?"

"What are convulsions?" I ask.

"Things that might make you look like a chicken, Reggie!"

She pauses for a moment, catching her breath and waiting for me to speak, but before I can figure out what on earth to say she carries on.

"Not only did you carry on with this ridiculous hobby after I told you not to, you thought you would get away with THIS." She is so worked up, I can see the veins in her neck getting bigger and I start worrying that they might pop and then that would all be my fault too.

"The school now have their eye on you. Luckily for you, I told them that it was a phase and it's harmless, but when they told me that you had also called a teacher boring, there was nothing I could do. You are in detention every lunchtime for a week."

"Not lunchtime!" I shout. I need my lunchtimes with the gang. I need to hypnotize the school. I've only just found it. I can't have it taken away now.

Then Dad's voice speaks loudly and clearly. "Do the crime, do the time, Reggie. Now I want you to apologize to your mother and then I want you to promise me that you will knock off this hypnosis thing. Get yourself a proper hobby like footy or something."

I'm about to argue, to try and explain that it is a proper hobby and that I am good at it. That it's the only thing that has ever got me friends. But I see his face and I know he won't get it.

"Sorry, Mum," I say, and then, "I promise." But I know that the gang won't let me give up that easily. Not when there is money to be made.

"Now get upstairs and write a letter saying sorry and get well soon to Mr Gray."

"What? But Dad's back," I moan.

"Don't even think about arguing, Reggie Houser," Mum says, and Dad nods sadly.

"You brought it on yourself, Reg," he says.

I sigh and slope up to my room.

It's not fair.

When I'm sitting on my bed with a piece of paper resting on one of my favourite mind-control books, I drift off as soon as I've written the words "Dear Mr Gray" and start thinking about what happened in assembly. The feeling of the whole room being alive like that, the energy and excitement of so many people, and all because of me.

I leaf through the book until I get to a page that makes me stop and let my eyes rest on the opening words.

Mass hypnosis is what happens when a clear message is stated and repeated so that it implicitly makes sense and is accepted by the group.

Mum managed to convince the school that Mr Gray was just poorly, that what he was doing on stage was just groaning or coughing. It's like she has almost hypnotized them too. If they believe that and we all believed he was a chicken, it's hard to even know what's real when people can believe anything they want to.

I think about that moment in the assembly hall. I

shouted the words, "It's chicken time!" and Mr Gray became a chicken. It was clear to everyone. It was as real as the book in my hand or the breath in my body. Or was it? Did me shouting the word chicken make the kids think or accept that everything Mr Gray did looked more chicken-like than it actually did? Was he clucking or was he groaning? Were his arms wings or were they holding his stomach? Did everyone just go along with what I said? Did I actually hypnotize the whole room rather than turning Mr Gray into a bird?

All the questions and confusion hurt my head and I can't think straight. I wish there was someone I could talk to about it all. Someone who would be honest with me and tell me the truth about hypnosis and how it all works. Whether it's just a lot of tricks, coincidences and confidence or whether it's as real and powerful as it feels in the moment. I so desperately want it to be real. It's real for me. I've made myself happier and people really want to be my friend. But no one else can ever understand what it feels like to do it. The place my brain goes to, the confidence I have when I'm telling someone what to do or how to breathe.

Then it hits me. There *is* someone I can talk to. Someone that I can ask all of these questions. Michael

Gareth. I just need to find him! I immediately drop my "Dear Mr Gray" paper and pick up my phone, typing in the name. Hoping to see a picture of his face.

His website looks like it's been made by a kid. It's one page with some cheesy photos of him on boats and stages. I can't find anything helpful until I scroll to the bottom and see a button. "Send Michael Gareth a message." I smile and click.

Dear Michael Gareth,

My name is Reggie Houser. We met at a show you did at Trontin's holiday park. Since then I have been practising my mind control and hypnotism non-stop. I have managed to hypnotize my neighbours' dog, three toddlers who my mum looks after, my head teacher (which got me into loads of trouble!), and lots of kids at school.

I love how it feels when someone is listening to my low voice and I like watching their eyelids get heavy.

I'm starting to wonder though, if it's all real? Sometimes some of the things I do are just silly tricks and other times, when I think I have properly hypnotized someone, it turns

174

out that they were only going along with it or were not hypnotized at all.

I don't know anyone else I can ask. My mum wants me to give it up as she thinks it's dangerous. What do you think? Is it as magical as it feels?

Kind regards,
Reggie Houser

P.S. What did you do when you hypnotized me, when I brought you the cake? I never found out so I guess it must not have worked.

I click send and lie back on my bed, exhausted from all the thinking. Maybe rolling down the hill was simpler than this. When I think about the sensation of rolling I have an urge to run out of the door and find the biggest hill I can. But I have grown out of that now, so I squash down the feeling and try something else to calm my brain down.

As I'm lying there, noticing how much warmer my breath is on the way out than on the way in, my phone beeps and I see a message. I never get messages. You have to have friends to get messages. I feel a tingle of excitement as I pick up the phone. I open it to see a picture of Blane's face looking out beyond two sets of middle fingers. I wonder if his mum knows that he uses a sweary photo as his profile picture. Maybe she doesn't care. Under his angry-looking face are the words:

> Meet at Londis in half an hour.
> Got a plan.

My heart beats a bit faster as I read the words. I'm not sure Mum will let me out, but I run downstairs. I'm going to meet my mates at Londis. This is what normal kids do!

She looks up as I walk into the kitchen. "You finished?"

"Finished what?" I ask, knowing from her sigh that I've forgotten something.

"Why did you go upstairs, Reggie?"

"Because you told me to?"

"What did I ask you to do?"

I look at her blankly, not knowing why I'm being so annoying. I can see Dad pottering about in the garden. As I look at him testing the brakes on my bike and taking a drink of tea, I wonder if he likes coming home. As soon as he gets here, he goes outside. It's like he doesn't really know what to do with a house. I don't know if it's because he is so used to being in a hotel room for his work or if he was always like this. Mum once said that he was like a wild dog and would probably be happier in a kennel.

"Reggie!" Mum snaps, bringing me back into the moment.

"Can I go out?" I ask, completely forgetting that I was meant to be answering her question.

"No! Get upstairs right now and write a letter apologizing to Mr Gray!"

"Oh, the letter!" I say. "Sorry, I got distracted. I forgot."

"Well, get as distracted as you like. You are not leaving this house until you've done it."

I run back upstairs and grab the paper. I quickly scribble a note underneath the words "Dear Mr Gray".

I am really sorry for trying to hypnotize you. I won't do it again.
Reggie Houser

As I'm about to fold it in half I look at how short it is and add:

P.S. Get well soon.

I run back downstairs past Mum and as I'm getting my shoes on, she holds out her hand, demanding to look at the paper. When she reads it, she rolls her eyes.

"Not exactly setting the world on fire, but it will do, I suppose. Where are you going?"

"I'm going to take it to school now, so he gets it as soon as possible." Then before she can turn her confused expression into a question, I dash through the front door.

I wonder what the gang have planned. I feel excited as I run down the road. As I slow down and catch my breath, I hope that I'm not going to get into any more trouble. Then a beep and a buzz and a picture pops up on my phone of Blane and the gang outside Londis, saying:

We are here.

I smile and start running and when Mr Richards from Number 12 walks past me, I shout, "I'm going to meet my mates!"

DO TRY THIS AT HOME!

PREDICTION TIME

Go and get nine small items and lay them out on a table. Write the name of one of the items on a piece of paper and hide it somewhere. Find a willing volunteer. (By now, your regular volunteer may roll their eyes and groan as you approach them with another trick. Ignore this and force them to join in against their will.) Point at two items — NOT THE ITEM ON THE PAPER — and ask the reluctant volunteer to eliminate one of them. Now they do the same and you eliminate one, always keeping the chosen item safe. Keep going until only the chosen item remains. You can then reveal your prediction. (If you can make it seem like you have found the prediction in their ear even better.)

CHAPTER SEVENTEEN

Remember to chew your food. Last time you had a Mars bar, you shoved it in your mouth in one go and ended up choking. SLOW DOWN.

Approaching Londis, I see them leaning against the wall. Blane is doing a wheelie on his bike and nearly topples over backwards, making the others cackle and hold their sides.

I wave when they see me and Vince shouts, "Reggie Houser, the best hypnotist in the world!" The others shush him and look towards the shop.

When I reach them they bundle me around the corner and into a side street.

"So, Reggie Roo Roo, we've been thinking."

I wait, wondering what they're going to say.

"Today, when you told that Year Eight kid to empty his bag all over the floor every time the bell rang, I had a brilliant idea."

Blane keeps saying how brilliant the idea is but I'm not sure that I believe him.

"If you can make someone empty their bag, you can make them give you the stuff that's in it, right?"

"I guess so. It depends how suggestible they are though."

"But, in theory, you could make someone give you anything, right?"

"It depends who they are," I say again, feeling annoyed that they don't seem to care about how it all works. They aren't bothered that I don't know if it even really does work.

"So, if you go into the shop," Blane carries on, "you could get the old hag in there to give you anything for free."

"No!" I say immediately, panic filling my body. I'm not going to steal something. This feels bad. Different to messing about at school and hypnotizing kids and teachers. This is real.

"Reggie, chill out!" says Max.

"We were just wanting to see if you *could* do it,

that's all. We're not expecting you to empty the till or anything. Start small."

"Yeah," adds Vince. "Get us something little."

"Just a Freddo or something. It won't bankrupt her and she'll never know. Don't you want to see if you can do it?"

"Not really," I say, ignoring the fact that just hearing the word Freddo made my mouth water and now all I can think of is eating one.

Max puts his arm around me. "Listen, buddy, it's not like we haven't got money, is it? We made a fortune today. You can just test your skills, try it out, and if it works we can go back and pay her later. No harm done."

"Well, if we pay her back," I say, still unsure. Maybe it would be a good test to see if this stuff works in the real world. It's not stealing if I pay her back, is it?

"Of course, Reggie. Go and do your stuff. We'll wait here."

I hesitate and then feel Blane's hand on my back pushing me towards the main road.

How would I even do this? I could take the Freddo to the till and stare her in the eyes and tell her that I have paid and hope she is convinced. I could try a fast hypnotic induction and hope that she sleeps as I dash out of the door. I could suggest that all Freddos are free today, that it's in the newspapers and everything. I could just use my fiver and pay for it and then tell the gang that I did it. But there is a part of me that wants to see if I can do it. To see what happens.

As my feet carry me towards the door, I decide on the first option. Just take it to the till, get eye contact, say thank you and leave. No money just a polite and harmless trick. She will have had so many people at the till today that the repetition of taking money will make her believe that she has taken my money – or that's what I'm hoping.

I stand, staring at the chocolate, and occasionally glancing at the lady behind the till. She has a tired but stern expression and I instantly feel like she would not be very suggestible. I look out to the street and see a bike wheel. They're waiting for me. I have to give this a go, and the more nervous I am the less likely it will be to work. Confidence is the biggest part of mind control.

"Hello," says the lady when I put the Freddo down.

"Hi," I say, looking directly into her eyes.

She looks at me and is slightly taken aback by my direct gaze but then beeps the frog and says, "Forty-nine pence, please, love."

My heart is galloping in my chest and I almost wimp out but then as I lock eyes with her again a huge sense of calm washes over me and I feel like I could do anything.

"Thank you," I say, sliding my hand on to the counter and taking the Freddo bar, eyes still locked on hers.

As I turn towards the door, I think I've done it but seconds later I hear her voice.

"Excuse me, young man," she says. "You didn't pay."

I almost choke but manage to say, "I did. I gave you two twenty ps and some coppers." As her face fills with confusion and she opens her till, I bottle it and run out the door.

"Go!" I scream at the gang. "Run!"

As we are sprinting down the side street, I hear the shouts of the lady at the shop follow us down the road and into an alley where we all collapse, breathing hard. Our eyes are wide and pupils dilated, sweat on our foreheads and fear in our bodies, but as we all slump to the floor, we start laughing hard. The fear suddenly turning to joy. The feeling reminds me of being at the bottom of the hill. A dizzy brain overwhelming all the other feelings.

"That was a rush!" Vince says, and we all nod our agreement, catching our breath between giggles.

"Well, that was just a warm-up," says Blane. "We've got even bigger plans for you, Reggie."

Hearing the sound of Blane's voice makes the feeling of elation and adrenaline suddenly drop and I instantly feel sick and scared. If Mum ever found out about me stealing she would be so sad and disappointed. In my mind I see the shop lady's face and eyes as she looked into mine from behind the till. What have I done? What will they ask me to do next? Before the panic really sets in, Oscar snaps me out of it.

"We're going down the skate park tomorrow if you want to come?"

Then Max grabs Oscar into a big, fake hug.

"It's Oscar Woscar and Vincey Wincey's birthdays tomorrow," he says, messing Oscar's hair up and pinching Vince's cheeks.

No one has ever invited me to their birthday before or to the skate park. I used to go and watch the older kids doing flips and tricks and wish I was like them. Maybe being a thief is worth it after all. I smile and nod.

"See you in the park at eleven?" Oscar says.

"I won't have time to get you both a present," I say.

Blane and Max both say, "Ahhhh," and grab me into a big fake hug which feels a bit too tight to be as fun as it looks.

"Reggie Weggie is so sweet, he thinks he's going to a birthday party with balloons and cake."

"We haven't got them a present and we've known them all our life!" They all laugh and I'm a bit confused. The way they are so mean to each other feels a bit sad but they all seem to enjoy it.

Oscar looks at my confused face. "You can turn Vince into a birthday hippopotamus for me and tie him up in a bow." He laughs and Vince punches him on the arm.

This is really happening now. I'm actually one of them. This is how it feels to be laughing and wrestling and part of a gang.

As I walk home, I put my hands into my pockets. In one side I feel the undelivered apology to Mr Gray, and in the other the Freddo. It's almost like feeling the two different directions my life could take. If I post the letter I could make all of this go away. Mum being angry, getting into trouble at school. I could become a good kid. Go back to sitting next to Lily. Ditch the gang. Stop controlling minds, just like Mum wants. The idea of losing my first real friends makes me feel sad.

Then my fingers feel the shape of the chocolate through the wrapper. I pull out the stolen frog and look at it. A slight rush of excitement passes through me at the memory of running out of the shop. The feeling of power that I had for a brief moment as I looked into her eyes. The feeling of being part of something. Having proper mates and making things happen.

I pass a bin and stop, pulling out the letter and then holding it beside the chocolate bar. I'm scared about what the gang might ask me to do next. Stealing a Freddo was really bad, I know, and they seemed to think it was nothing. Just a joke. But I have a gang for the first time in my life. I have somewhere to go and people who don't think I'm annoying. They need me.

I take one last look at the letter and the chocolate, deciding which one I should forget about. Which route I'm going to go down. I hover the frog over the bin as I think about Mum and Dad at home, but then at the last minute I think about the taste of the sweet chocolate and I throw the letter inside the bin, open the chocolate and shove it in my mouth before I have the chance to feel bad about it.

Dad is still wearing his work trousers and standing awkwardly in the kitchen when I get back. He wears his building trousers all the time, even when there is no building to do. Mum always says my ADHD comes from him. She says he can't sit still long enough to take his shoes off.

"Did you post it?" Mum asks.

"Yeah," I lie. Looking her in the eyes and making sure I don't give away my secret by looking up to the right. Apparently if you are telling the truth you look to the left, that's what one website said. Another one said it was a load of old rubbish, but I might as well not risk it.

"Kai is coming over for tea," Mum purrs. She looks really happy. I'm glad that she's smiling, but a part of me knows that it's because she doesn't like it when it's just me and her. I'm not enough to make her happy. That thought makes me sad and I turn and take out my frustration on Dad for no other reason than I have no idea what else to do with it.

"Why are you lurking in the kitchen, Dad?" I say with a snarl. "You never sit down, it's weird." He doesn't bite and just laughs.

"You're weird," he says, playing our old game of insults, expecting me to say it back. Maybe a year ago, I would have. Maybe even a few weeks ago, I would, and we would have said it over and over again until he got me in a headlock and we wrestled each other to the ground. Today I don't feel like it though, so I just turn and head to my room.

DO TRY THIS AT HOME!

RED HAMMER

Write the words red hammer on a piece of paper. Now hide it and ask someone the following questions quickly one after the other. Don't let them think too long.

- What day is Christmas?
- What is 5 × 3?
- What year was it 10 years ago?
- How many sides does a stop sign have?
- What are hamburgers made of?
- What side of the road do they drive on in London?
- Quick: think of a colour and a tool!

If they say red hammer you can reveal your red hammer. If not, say, "Quick look, there is a bearded man riding on

a huge dog's back." Then run as fast as
your little legs will carry you.

CHAPTER EIGHTEEN

GO WHEREVER YOU WANT

If you want Mum to let you go somewhere, tell her you are meeting friends. She will be so happy that you actually have any friends, she'll let you go anywhere.

On Saturday morning I shove some Shreddies into my mouth and ask Mum if I'm allowed to go to the park. She looks at me over the cereal box.

"Who are you going with?" she asks suspiciously.

"My new mates from school."

She can't help but smile and I know immediately she will let me go.

"I shouldn't really be letting you have any fun at

all after what you did at school to that poor man, but if you tell me all about your new friends then I will think about it."

I tell her that they are cousins and they like football and riding bikes. I tell her that they think I'm funny and that it's Oscar and Vince's birthday. When I say that, she looks all excited. In primary school Mum used to get so sad when I didn't get invited to parties. Once Isla handed out invites to every single kid in the class apart from me. Mum got so angry. She called Isla's mum and shouted about kindness but I still didn't get an invite.

I kind of wish I hadn't mentioned the birthday as she starts buzzing around saying I need to take something and talking about what I'm wearing. I remember Max and Blane squeezing me when I mentioned presents.

"Mum, I don't think it's like that. It's not a party, we are just going to the skate park. We are too old for parties now, we're just going to hang out."

"Ridiculous. A birthday is a birthday. They need a present."

After she has rummaged around in the drawer where the wrapping paper is, she sighs.

"I wish you had given me more notice, Reggie."

"They only asked me yesterday."

She gets a fiver out of her wallet and hands it to me.

"Well, go to Londis on your way and get some chocolate."

I try to keep my face normal looking even though I can feel the colour draining from it.

"OK, thanks," I say as I take the money, knowing that I am not going anywhere near Londis ever again.

I realize now that when the gang said we could pay the shop lady back they probably knew that wouldn't happen. I couldn't go there and face her again, not now. Guilt surges through my body but I tell myself that it's only a Freddo and I won't ever need to go into Londis again anyway.

As I walk into the park, carrying my old skateboard under my arm, I wonder if there will be anyone else there. I know they made out like birthdays were babyish but Oscar and Vince might have told some of the lads at school or some of their family might be here. When I get to the skate park there is no one there and I feel instantly sad and scared that they have changed their minds about me. I look at my phone and there's nothing from them. It's only just eleven though, so I sit in the spot that I used to sit in. I watch a tiny little boy running up and down the ramps with his mum anxiously watching as he speeds up down the hills.

"Hi, Reggie!" a high voice calls and it takes me a minute to see where it's coming from. A waving arm on the other side of the skate park draws my attention and then I see her. Lily is standing there waving wildly at me. She looks even tinier and younger than usual. My heart sinks. This is the last thing I need. I do a small wave and then get out my phone to see if the lads have sent anything. I'm hoping that Lily will get the hint and go away, but when I risk a glance up from the screen she is almost next to me.

"Hi, Reggie," she says, smiling at me. "You here on your own?"

"No, I'm waiting for my mates."

"Those horrible boys?"

Before I can answer I see Oscar and the gang standing behind Lily. They put their fingers to their lips and sneak up on her. When they get close enough they all jump out and grab her shoulders, shouting and getting in her face. She screams and they all laugh.

I want Lily to get up and go. For some reason I'm worried about her. She's so small and innocent and seeing the look on the boys' faces makes a rush of fear surge through my chest. I want her to get away from them now, but she stays sitting next to me, scowling at the gang.

"You brought your girlfriend, Reggie?" Max snarls.

"She was definitely not invited," Blane adds.

I want this to stop. It doesn't feel good at all.

"Happy birthday," I say, trying to change the subject.

"Did you bring them a present?" Blane asks Lily, but I interrupt quickly.

"My mum gave me a fiver to get some…"

"You brought them a fiver? That's so sweet." Blane holds his hand out and so I get the crumpled note out of my pocket and hand it to him.

"Happy birthday," Blane says. "This is from all of us. Now, boys, your main present is Reggie Weggie here hypnotizing someone. Who would you like him to hypnotize first?"

This feels bad. It's so different to last night. Their voices are more threatening and Lily sitting here makes me feel scared. I try to catch her eye to tell her to go. I look at the skate park to see who's around, but the little boy and his mum are walking away towards the duck pond. Blane carries on.

"You could turn Vince into a hippo or make Max

think he's the king or…" He pauses and smiles a horrible smile as he leans in towards Lily. "You could hypnotize your girlfriend here. What do you reckon, lads?"

"He's not hypnotizing me," Lily says and starts to stand, but as she does Blane holds her shoulders down so she can't get up.

"That's not up to you, princess. Unless it's your birthday too."

I can see Lily's face change as she feels his hands pressing down on her shoulders. She looks terrified.

"What should he make her do?" Max asks and Oscar looks unsure. They are all still laughing and smiling but the energy in the air is scary. I have never felt anything like it before. Lily squirms and tries to get away but Blane is far too strong. This is not fun. This is not what being in a gang should feel like at all. I have to do something. Lily should never have come over here.

"OK, let her go," I say, trying to keep my voice light, but the fear in it is clear. "I will turn Vince into a hippo."

"I think we've moved on from that idea, Reg. We want you to hypnotize your girlfriend." They all wait for me to start.

Every book, every podcast, every website has said that you should only hypnotize people who want to be hypnotized. I think about Mr Gray and the woman in the shop last night. She didn't want to be robbed and I did it anyway and that ended up being OK. Maybe this will be fine too. Maybe I'm overreacting. They're all just messing about after all, aren't they? Then as I am about to click my fingers, I look into Lily's wide eyes and see the fear in them. I can't do this.

"No," I whisper.

"What?" Blane asks.

I can't look at him so I look at the floor.

"No!" I say again, louder this time.

As he turns on me he let's go of Lily's shoulders and she scrambles to her feet.

"Run!" I whisper and she hesitates, looking worried for me, wondering if she should try and help me. "Run!" I shout at her. Then she makes her decision and runs.

The boys surround me.

"Well, that wasn't a very nice birthday present, was it? You might have made Oscar cry. Oscar, are you crying?" Oscar pretends to cry and they all laugh. I still don't know how bad this is. What would they have made Lily do? Why does it feel so bad? I need it to go back to being fun.

"Shall I hypnotize Vince?" I say weakly.

"Nah, that's a bit boring, Reg. We are thinking up a brilliant plan for you but I'll be honest, what has happened today is making me worry about you. Do you even want to be in this gang?"

"Yes," I say, not even knowing if that's true any more.

"Well, the next thing we ask you to do you'd better do it. OK?"

"Yeah," I say, nodding.

"Whatever we ask, you will do it?"

"I promise."

DO TRY THIS AT HOME!

CARROT

This is a weird one. (It doesn't work 100% of the time, but when it does it feels so good that it's worth the embarrassment when it fails miserably.) Take a piece of paper and write the word carrot on it. Give it to your volunteer — again, a human volunteer is a must for this one, unless you have a talking dog who can do maths. Make sure they don't look at the paper. Ask them what 1+1 is. Then 2+2, 3+3 and so on until you get to 8+8. Then tell them to think of a vegetable. Most of the time they will say carrot. If they do, tell them to look at the paper. (If they say potato or aubergine then shout, "Look over there, a lollipop." Then turn and run.)

CHAPTER NINETEEN

WAYS TO GET BACK TO SLEEP

— Count your breath to ten then go back to one and start again. (Basically bore yourself to sleep.)

— Make sure your wrists and ankles are snuggly warm.

— Play the weird playlist of birds singing. (Don't play the ocean one again — remember, you did a bit of a wee that night.)

— Write down all the thoughts in your brain and when you run out, try to sleep. (If the thoughts just keep coming don't stay up writing them down until the morning or Mum will get cross again.)

    – Lavender spray. Make sure the nozzle is not pointing at your face.

That night I can't sleep at all. My brain is full of thoughts and pictures of Lily's scared face, the lady in the shop and the gang in the alleyway. Thoughts about what they will ask me to do next. No amount of breathing or self-hypnosis will stop it from whirring. At about three o'clock in the morning, I feel like I might explode. I have to do something. I pick up my phone and find Lily on Snapchat.

    I'm sorry. I hope you are ok.

I press send and wait for a while but no one in the world is awake at this time so I give up and silently head downstairs to get some milk and toast.

    I've tried loads of things to help me sleep over the years. Apparently not sleeping is an ADHD thing. When nothing works, the only option is to get up and have milk and toast and then go back and try again.

    The kitchen feels extra quiet in the middle of the night and the sound of the toast popping makes me jump. As I turn around, I nearly scream when I see

Dad standing in the doorway in his scruffy tracksuit. I'm so used to him being away that I'm not expecting to see him in the doorway. Dad doesn't sleep either. When I was little we used to make eggy bread in the middle of the night. When he's away it feels weird in the kitchen at night knowing I will be on my own. Once I'm over the shock of seeing him I smile and feel so happy that he's here.

"Couldn't sleep, buddy?" he asks quietly. I shake my head and go and sit on the worn-out armchair, balancing my toast on my knee.

"Me neither," he says as he puts the kettle on.

I watch him as he gets a mug out and potters around the kitchen. He looks different to how Mum would look in the middle of the night. He's not rubbing his eyes or yawning. He's like me. We are both awake and buzzy and busy and all the other things everyone calls me. A question pops into my brain and before I can stop it, it spills out of my mouth.

"Do you think you've got ADHD, Dad?" I ask.

"What are you on about?"

"Maybe I get it from you."

"Don't be blaming me, kid!"

"I'm not," I say quickly. "I just mean the way you

203

are. We are a bit the same. We are both awake, aren't we?"

He laughs and shrugs.

"There wasn't such a thing when I was a kid. Seems to be everywhere nowadays. No point me finding out at my age, even if I did have it."

"What's age got to do with it?" I ask, taking a bite, crumbs landing on my chest.

"Well, I'm all right, aren't I? I've managed. What difference would it make?"

"Maybe if you knew you could find ways to make it easier. Take some tablets, or I could teach you self-hypnosis." Then, hesitating, I add, "Then you might be able to be in the house a bit more. You might not be awake at three in the morning. You might enjoy being with us."

"I love being with you, Reg. I just like being busy, that's all. There's nothing wrong with that, is there?"

"No, I guess not." He's right, being busy is fine, but there is something about the expression on his face, the way that he's busy that makes me realize something that I've never thought about Dad before. All of his half-finished projects, pottering, working away and never sitting down make him different. Just like me. Even at work with his mates with nicknames,

I bet he doesn't sit and talk and listen to them. I think about today and how even as I was laughing with the gang, how my brain was already thinking about a million other things and feeling guilty for everything. For the first time I realize that even with a gang, you can still be alone.

"It just sometimes looks a bit lonely, that's all, Dad."

He looks confused when I say this, like he doesn't really know what to do. I look at him and I know in that moment that he is lonely, like me. But even worse than me, because he doesn't even know it, let alone the reason why. He doesn't really know how to be part of the family, or part of anything, and that's why he lives like he does. Out of a rucksack. On the road.

I don't want to be alone like that when I'm older. Pretending to have great mates by calling them by their surnames, but probably never really talking about anything important with them. I want to learn how to be still and listen properly. I want to teach my brain how to actually hear what people are saying to me and not fog up or accidentally listen to everything else in the room. I want to find proper friends who really get me and like the same things as I do. Not friends who scare me and make me do things that

I don't want to do. I want someone who would roll down a hill with me or let me talk about mind control until I run out of words.

As I chomp through my toast and look at Dad's sad face I know deep down that Blane, Max, Vince and Oscar are not those people. They won't make me a better version of myself. They're not my friends. Then I feel sadder than Dad looks, as I realize that none of that matters because at the moment they're all I've got.

On Monday morning, after spending the whole of Sunday worrying and checking my phone, I have had barely any sleep all weekend. I feel the familiar buzzing feeling of the extra energy that I seem to find when I've had no sleep. I know people say that you need sleep to have energy but that's definitely not true for me. I have way more energy when I've been up all night.

Mum frowns at me when I manage to drop all of the cereal boxes as I take the Shreddies from the cupboard. Cornflakes spill on to the floor and I freeze.

"Pick them up, then!" she says, and when I do even

more cereal manages to land on the tiles as I hold the box the wrong way round.

"For goodness' sake, Reggie. Just leave it!"

"Sorry, Mum," I say.

I get halfway down the road before realizing I've forgotten my school bag. When I have it on my back and am walking down the road for the second time, I look down and notice that I am wearing odd shoes. I'm not sure if I should turn back again and risk Mum sighing and huffing. I'll be late for school if I do. Maybe I should just carry on and hope that no one notices.

I stop walking and am stuck with indecision. Walking a couple of steps in one direction and then changing my mind and turning the other way. One shoe is a black school shoe, the other is an old grey trainer with a hole in the toe. I'm not sure how I managed to mix them up. I wiggle my toes and see my green sock poking out. Do people notice other people's feet? I don't think I do. I would never look at people's shoes. I try to remember what any of the gang were wearing on their feet yesterday and I can't. Surely that's proof that no one will notice. I keep walking towards school and then an old lady walks past and looks down at my feet, so I turn back the other way towards home and then stop. Frozen again.

When I look at the time I gasp. I have been standing there, unable to decide what to do, for ten minutes. I'm going to be so late. I head towards school and forget about my odd feet.

When I get there, I peek in through my form room door and see everyone sitting listening to the teacher. I know I'll get in trouble, so I don't go in. Even though somewhere deep down I know I'm only making it worse by waiting, getting later with every breath.

Lily looks up from her desk and sees me and I feel instant guilt and shame, but she smiles. She gestures, telling me to come in, but I shake my head. She looks at me, confused, but then seems to understand and does something so kind that it almost takes my breath away. She puts up her hand and then carries a book to the front of the class, asking the teacher to look at it. With her back to me she motions behind telling me to come in and sit down, while blocking the teacher's view of the door. When I am sitting in my old spot at her desk she comes and plonks herself cheerfully next to me and smiles. I flush bright red.

"You're welcome," she whispers, adding with a smile, "Why have you got odd shoes on?"

At break time I don't run away from Lily like I normally do. She comes and sits with me on the bench by the netball court. I'm kind of surprised that she's still bothering with me after everything that's happened. As I'm thinking about how she's actually pretty tough and trying to find words for all of the things that I should say to her, to tell her that what happened yesterday was not OK and that she was right all along about the gang, I notice that she has glitter and stars in her hair.

"Did your sister do that?" I ask.

"Yeah."

"It's cool," I say, not fully meaning it. The stars kind of make my eyes go blurry and my brain hurt just looking at them, but I want to be nice.

Then she leans over and whispers, "I've never told anyone this, but I actually would rather just have short hair or at least just put it up in a pony and be done with it, but my sister likes doing it and my mum thinks I look pretty, so I just let them brush and style and spray me every morning."

"What would they say if you told them?" I ask, interested now in the idea that she would just let this happen every day and never say anything.

"They would feel sad, I guess. Anyway, my hair is a total frizzball if I don't do anything to it." Then she pauses and smiles as if she's waiting for me to say something. When I don't, she says, "Now it's your turn to tell me something."

"What?" I ask.

"Tell me something. A secret or something that you have never told anyone."

Before I can stop them, the words pop out of my mouth.

"I stole a Freddo bar."

Lily gasps and covers her mouth. "Why?" she says in a whisper.

"Because they told me to," I say quietly.

"You need to get away from them."

"I don't think it's that easy. They have got more plans for me."

"Just say no!" she says in an almost shout.

"How about you 'just say no' to being turned into a human Christmas tree every day?" I shout back. When she slumps and frowns, I smile. "It's not that easy, is it?" Then we both sit, our brains whirring and wondering what an earth we should do.

After a few minutes of silence Lily whispers, "If you need me to help, you know where I am."

"Thanks, Lily," I say, feeling the sun poking through the cloud and warming my face.

At lunch, I'm heading to detention when Blane and Max turn into the corridor.

"Wrong way, Reggie. We've got customers waiting," says Blane.

"We need to tell you the plan," adds Max.

"I'm in detention all week," I say. "We need to be more careful. It's probably best to stop for a while."

"Meet us after school by the gates, then," Blane says and pats me hard on the back. As they walk away, I hear them talking about if they can still charge everyone a pound even though I'm not there. I sigh. Having a gang is not really what I'd hoped it would be like. I walk into detention and a room full of annoyed-looking kids look up at me and down to my shoes and all start giggling. So much for no one noticing. People giggling at me now feels different though. They all still think I'm the school hero so they are giggling but they are also waving, and I can hear them saying my name. I think I can probably get away with odd shoes.

As we sit there in the silence of detention,

all pretending to do our homework, the teacher occasionally looks up from her desk and glares at us. It looks as though she is so disgusted by us that she actually hates us. Some teachers look so unhappy, I really do wonder why they do it. As I'm staring out of the window, she tells us that she's going to the school office and will be back in a few minutes. A thought to ease the boredom pops into my brain and I can't not do it. It's one of those ideas that makes me smile and simply cannot just stay inside my brain. It has to go from being a thought to being real. It has to happen, it's like I have no choice.

I stand up and go to the front of the class, the bored detention kids all looking at me wondering what's going to happen.

"What you doing, Reg?"

"Hypnotize us, Reggie!"

I hold up my finger and tell them to follow it. They all do exactly what I say. It's the perfect setting, a room full of bored kids. They will all be so suggestible. As I lower my finger I tell them to close their eyes and as I raise it they open them.

"Every time your eyes close it gets harder and harder to open them," I say in my calm, confident voice. As all of the eyes close for the last time I look out at the room full of lolling heads. This is so cool. I've read up loads on mass hypnosis, but this is better than I thought it would be; every single kid looks totally under my spell. I think about what I want them all to do.

"When the teacher comes back, if she glares at you, you will cry. Not a small, little cry but big, huge sobs, like a wailing baby." I laugh to myself imagining what is about to happen and then as I look down at my feet I add one more instruction. "When you open your eyes, you will swap a single shoe with another kid. Having odd shoes is the next big thing. You will think you are so cool, you will show off your mismatched shoes to everyone."

By the time the teacher comes back the shoes have all been swapped and it doesn't take long for kids to start crying. By the end of lunch, the teacher looks completely frazzled and the kids leaving detention with odd feet and tears streaming down their faces get quite a lot of attention. I skip out the door and bump straight into Lily who is looking at me suspiciously.

"What did you do?"

"Nothing!" I say innocently. "I just made detention a bit more interesting, that's all."

After school the gang are waiting by the gates,

and I almost spit my drink out when I see that they have odd shoes on. The idea must have spread! They launch straight into the new plan. Vince says he watched some show on telly that gave him the idea. They show me videos that they have made on their phones of a man leaving the bank. I recognize the high street. At first I'm confused, not really knowing what they are saying. Their voices are overlapping in excitement.

"It'll be easy, Reggie!"

"It's not stealing if he gives it to you, is it?"

"We will be rich."

"He won't even remember you."

They have a map drawn up of the street and where the van is parked, where they will hide and what they want me to do. This is insane. What are they talking about? I can't believe they have discussed this and planned it and actually expect me to do it. I can feel my chest getting tight and eyes blurring as they talk faster and faster in more excited voices.

None of them seem to care that I'm not listening, that I can barely breathe. None of them care that I don't want anything to do with this plan. I want to stop the world from turning and jump off. I want to go back to primary school where I got into trouble for farting. I don't even want my mind-control skills any more, not if this is what happens. I don't want to hypnotize anyone ever again, not if it means I have to rob a bank.

As they are still talking, explaining the details, I turn and run. I run so fast in my odd shoes that I nearly fall but pick myself up and keep on running. I hear them chasing me, shouting after me that I am not getting out of it.

"We'll kill you, Reggie, if you don't do it." But I keep running. My chest exploding. My brain on fire. I want to keep running forever.

DO TRY THIS AT HOME!

LIFT ME UP

So you need a volunteer again, I'm afraid. When you have found one, stand facing them and ask them to lift you up by holding your waist or under your arms. You can make yourself feel lighter by tensing your body in preparation for the lift and even by giving a secret little push-off from the floor as they lift. They will feel strong and powerful.

Now ask them to lift you again, but this time tell them you are going to look into their eyes and drain their power. You can spout a load of old nonsense or pretend to hypnotize them, whatever you like to add drama. As they place their hands on your waist or under your arms, hold on to their forearms, slightly press into their elbow crease with your thumbs, and relax your body as they try and lift. They will not be able to lift you this time however strong they are. Feel the power!

CHAPTER TWENTY

REMEMBER TO ASK FOR HELP

When you get into a tizz and your brain stops working, ask someone to help you sort it out. Here is a list of people who might help:

- Mum

- Dad

- Kai

- Teachers

- Friends???

I'm so glad Dad's home. He will know what to do. As I run I just want to get back and hug him tight and

I can explain everything to him. Mum would just panic and scream and never let me out of the house again, but Dad will get it.

When I finally stop running and turn into my road, I see Barnaby and Dan standing at my open front door, chatting to Mum. As soon as Barnaby gets a sniff of me, he pulls his lead out of Dan's grasp and launches himself towards me.

On the floor and covered in slobber, I stroke his soft fur and for a moment forget the trouble I'm in and enjoy the simplicity that is a big, soppy dog.

"I thought you had him perfectly trained!" Dan says, smiling as he catches up with Barnaby.

"I do!" I say. "I told him to leap on me and lick me all over."

"Of course you did!" Dan laughs as he picks up the lead.

I get up and brush myself off, trying to hide my trainer foot.

"Did you need me to look after him again?" I ask.

"Not exactly," Dan says. "I was wondering if you could use your doggy skills on him and a few of his pals next weekend?"

Dan shows me a leaflet with fireworks on it. Some kind of street party celebrating the royal family.

"Barnaby is terrified of fireworks. So are all of his doggy buddies. I was hoping you could help?"

It feels so good being asked to help and do something useful. Something that doesn't involve lying or stealing. I nod and tell him that I can try.

"I think Barnaby misses you!" he says. "We have found someone else to let him out, but you are definitely his favourite."

I give Barnaby's ears a stroke as he gazes up at me with his big brown eyes.

"I miss you, Barnaby," I say, before waving them off down the street.

When I walk into the kitchen Mum and Dad look at me silently, and I know what they're thinking.

"It's only dogs! Surely I'm allowed to hypnotize dogs?!"

They smile and I know it's all right. Then I see Dad's bags by the door and my face drops.

"But you only just got home," I say, my chest tightening. I need him now more than ever. I have to talk to someone to get the thoughts out of my head and come up with a way out of this horrible mess. I want Dad to stay. To be a normal dad and be home every day.

"Another job, Reg. I've got to earn the pennies.

Now look after your mother, OK? She can't cope with any more stress from you, Reggie, do you understand?"

I nod sadly.

"No more nonsense."

He hugs me tight and then I watch him leave, ignoring the tears that are now streaming down my face. I have no idea what I'm going to do. I can't tell Mum, that's for sure. Images of the gang shouting after me down the road pop into my head, of them describing what they want me to do. I'm scared. What am I going to do? I can't go through with it, but I need a plan. A way to get out of it that will make them leave me alone forever. I wish there was someone else I could talk to. Someone who would be on my side.

Then in a flash it comes to me. She's been there all along. Trying to be my friend and I haven't let her in. Maybe now I need to ask for her help. I pick up my phone and find her on Snapchat. I press call and a picture of her with her hair in a twirly shape on top of her head pops up on to the screen.

"Hi, Reggie," Lily says, as if me calling is the most normal thing in the world.

"I was wondering if you could help me?" I say. "I'm in a bit of trouble."

"Where do you want to meet?" she says immediately, and in the space of a minute it's sorted. I'm heading to the park to meet Lily. My new and my only friend.

When I get there, she is swinging on the swing next to a little kid. As I look at her, there is something different but I can't figure out what it is. I look at her face harder. She is sticking her tongue out and making the boy laugh so much that snot's coming out of his nose. When she sees me, she jumps off the swing and waves to the little boy, making him giggle one more time.

"Do you know him?" I ask.

"No. We just made friends. I'm brilliant at making friends with little kids. Just not so good with kids our age."

There's something weird about Lily. Something childlike and innocent that makes me nervous for her, but at the same time jealous. It must be amazing to be so happy, so confident, that you can make friends just like that. I wonder why she hasn't been able to make friends at school yet. I've seen her trying to chat to some of the girls and they just ignore her or leave her out. We walk out of the play park and towards the field.

"So, what's up?" she says. "Or shall I try and read your mind for a change?"

She wiggles her fingers and pretends to be stealing my thoughts.

"You're in trouble," she says in this daft low voice. "You need my help?" For a second, I think she's actually doing it. It's true, after all, I am in trouble. Then I remember that is exactly what I told her on the phone. She carries on, her voice back to normal now. "Is it something to do with those horrible boys?"

I nod my head as we get to a bench and sit down and watch the dogs running around the field.

"Go on, then," she says eventually. "What do they want from you?"

I tell her everything. I tell her about the Freddo night and Michael Gareth. I tell her about Barnaby and the Squealers and about Mum and Dad and then about the gang and their plan. I talk for what feels like for ever and she just sits and listens, occasionally nodding her head. When I finally run out of words, I turn to her.

"I'm scared, Lily. I don't know what to do," I say.

She smiles and pulls a hidden pencil out of her hair and a notepad from her back pocket.

"We need to make a plan, Reggie. Everything is going to be fine. I promise."

"Thanks, Lily," I say, feeling a sense of relief wash over me. "I'm so sorry they treated you like that at the skate park. It was scary and I knew then that you were right; they *are* horrible boys. Boys that I don't want anything to do with any more."

"You don't need them. You've got me on your side now."

DO TRY THIS AT HOME!

WHAT DO COWS DRINK?

Ask someone the following questions. Point at something white and ask them what colour it is. Ask them what colour salt is. Ask them what colour snow is. Then ask them what cows drink. They will say milk. Then you get to call them a fool and a nincompoop, because cows don't drink milk — they make it! They drink water.

CHAPTER TWENTY-ONE

TAKE NOTES

If you want someone to think that you are intelligent and serious, then take notes. Detectives do it, journalists and lawyers do it. It makes you look very important.

As we sit hunched over Lily's notepad, trying to figure out what on earth we should do, the reality of just how bad this is hits me again in a wave.

"I had no idea they would go this far. I thought they were just a normal gang of naughty boys, not a bunch of criminals. Do you think I have to tell my mum or the police?" I start to panic about all the trouble I'm going to get in when Mum finds out.

Then I panic that if she tells the school and Blane and the gang get expelled or the police find them, they might actually hurt me. I look at Lily and know she is thinking the same things.

"I think that WE can totally fix it all, just me and you. Let's try and think of a plan that means no one robs anything, no grown-ups find out and the gang leave you alone forever. If that doesn't work then we will tell your mum. Deal?"

"Deal," I say.

She takes her pen and starts writing things down as we talk through everything until the sun has set and the park has emptied.

THE PLAN

1. Go to the shop and pay for the Freddo bar.
2. Tell the gang that you will go ahead with the plan.
3. Gather all the dogs.
4. Sit in wait at the bank.
5. Execute our awesome plan.
6. Hypnotize the gang.
7. Live happily ever after.
8. Always be nice to Lily.

"I'm not sure I can do all this, you know," I say. I'm terrified. "I don't even know most of the other dogs on the street. I've no idea if I can get them to do what I want. And what's number eight? I definitely can't guarantee that," I say, smiling.

Lily got very over-excited about our plan. At one point she suggested hypnotizing the gang into doing the robbery instead of me but that felt like too much.

"You said no one needs to rob anything! I don't want them to go to jail for the rest of their lives!" I said. "I just want them to stop. To leave me alone and maybe to get a bit of a shock. Stop them from doing stuff like this."

That's when she had the big idea.

All I need to do is convince the gang that we must carry out the robbery next Saturday afternoon. They said the security man leaves the bank every day at four p.m. so that should be fine. I just need to work on Barnaby. Hopefully the others will follow his lead. As I'm thinking about what will happen, imagining the dogs all copying each other, I remember how this whole thing started. I think about the slide at Trontin's and realizing I could make everyone clap their hands. That one person just copied another. How easy it is to control people.

Maybe that's what happened to me. I thought that

I was controlling everyone else, but really I was letting the gang control me. I let them suggest the Freddo thing because I wanted to be part of something. I wanted to clap along to their rhythm rather than finding my own. Maybe I'm the most suggestible person out there. More than anyone who plays along and becomes a pig or a rabbit for a while. I could have lost myself entirely if I had gone along with them. If I had been mesmerized by the group. Maybe I don't need a gang after all. I just need to know my own mind.

All of a sudden, I feel brighter and more positive. I smile at Lily and stand up, folding the piece of paper and putting it in my pocket as she places the pencil back into her hair.

"What else have you got in there?" I ask. She taps her nose and raises her eyebrows dramatically, as though she is hiding many secrets inside her ridiculous hairdo.

"Right, see you at school," she says as we go our separate ways.

"Do you think it will work?" I ask.

"Absolutely!" she says. I'm not totally sure that I believe her, but it's nice having a plan in my pocket and her on my side.

*

On Monday, Blane and the gang are as predictable as we had hoped.

"You are not getting out of it, Reggie," snarls Blane at break time, holding my neck so tightly I feel like he might crush it.

"Meet us at the gates after school, we are going to stake out the bank . . . you better be there, Reggie."

"I will. I promise."

I was worried that it would be hard for me to pretend. That me changing my mind would seem unrealistic, but the pain in my neck and the fear in my eyes makes me saying yes seem completely believable.

As I approach the gates at the end of the day, I can see Vince and Oscar having what looks like a full-on fight, but when I get nearer I realize it is supposed to be fun. They're wrestling each other to the ground, but Vince looks like he's enjoying it way more than Oscar. I picture myself being the one on the floor being punched and pummelled by them all and I feel sick and wobbly at the thought. When Max sees me he orders them to stop and they turn and head towards the high street.

My heart is pounding. I'm just going to let them do the talking and go along with everything they are saying. Only when they finish will I tell them what

I need them to do. When we get to a little side street where we can see the bank, we all crouch down and whisper. I think this makes us look way more obvious than if we all just stood and chatted like normal kids, but I don't say anything.

"So, the security guy is called Bob," says Max smugly. "I zoomed into his name badge." Max clearly thinks he is the brains of the group. "I thought you might need his name to hypnotize him better."

"Yes, very useful," I say, nodding my head and jotting it down.

"He arrives and parks in the same spot every day at three forty-five. He will be here any minute." Right on cue a van pulls up and a man who must be Bob gets out. They must have been down here watching this happen for days. Max carries on in a whisper. "Then he goes into the bank. He chats to the lady on the till and then goes into the back. Between three fifty-four and four zero three he comes out carrying two cases." We all wait. My heart is thumping and my stomach is churning wildly. Bob comes out exactly on time, carrying the two cases.

"They are full of cash," Blane whispers. "Must be thousands in there."

"All you have to do," Max continues, "is hypnotize

231

him into handing one over. We think you should wait until he gets back to the van, as he opens the back doors and usually sits for a minute once he has put the cases in. Look, he's doing it now. This would be your moment. So that's your chance."

We wait and silently watch as Bob gets into the van and drives away. I am counting my breathing to try and calm down my thumping heart and racing mind. They really mean this. They look deadly serious. Although Oscar and Vince look pretty scared too.

"Mmmm," I say, as though I am thinking hard about how I will do it. "Anything else?" I want them to feel like all of their hard work has paid off, like every tiny detail of what they know will be useful.

"What do you think Bob is like?" I say, chewing my pen. "Age, height, personality?"

"He gets out of breath easy," says Vince. "I think he's really unfit, so he won't be able to chase you – us." Vince has obviously been imagining being chased, which is good.

"He likes cake," adds Oscar. "Remember, he was eating that cream cake the other day when he got out and some went down his jacket."

"Ooh, that could be useful," I lie.

"How will you do it?" Vince asks, actually

interested now, but behind his question I sense some fear. Blane and Max are older and know how to mask any signs of weakness, but Oscar and Vince are out of their depth, I can see it. They are so desperate to please their older cousins, they would do anything, but they are in over their heads with this. Hopefully when I have finished with them they will never try anything like this again. I look at them all seriously.

"Right, I have an idea, but it's dangerous." They all lean in, hanging on my every word.

The next morning when I wake up from a fitful night of very little sleep, I find an email waiting for me from Michael Gareth:

Dear Reggie,

Thank you for your email. You are very young to be asking such big questions. I think you must be an excellent hypnotist and a rather remarkable boy.

The question of whether hypnosis is real is not one that I can answer easily. It is a question which has sat in my head, sometimes uncomfortably, for years. As I travel the world, turning people into Elvis on stage or making them fall in love with a teddy bear, the idea that they are somehow "just playing along" seems almost tragic. It has made me want to give up and get a "proper job". I think when I saw you in the summer I was having a crisis of confidence, as were you, but then something happened that helped me to believe again, and hopefully it will do the same for you.

Obviously you know that hypnosis is used for helping people with things they would like to change about themselves – giving up smoking, losing weight and sleeping better. This in itself could be enough to convince us that it is worthwhile even if it's not "real", but how about if it could change something about someone that they didn't even know they wanted to change? Something that was holding them back and making their life harder or more miserable? Something like hatred or prejudice.

I once did a stage show where I made two strangers believe they were falling in love. It was a silly little bit that got big laughs

and on this particular night I had chosen
two large, brutish-looking men who looked
more like they might fight each other than
love each other. (They were the types that
always got the biggest reaction from the
audience.) They had proved that they were
suggestible and as they gazed into each
other's eyes and started smiling and flirting
with one another I smugly enjoyed the
laughter and applause before finishing up
the show and heading home.

About two weeks later I got an email
from the wife of one of the brutish-looking
men saying that her husband had changed.
At first I was worried that someone might
be about to sue me, but she continued
and told me that before the show he had
struggled with anger issues, particularly
towards certain types of people. People
who looked like the man he fell in love with
under hypnosis. Since the show she had
seen him look at people more kindly and get
less aggressive in situations with other men.
She believed it was because he had been
hypnotized. I believe that it was because

235

he just needed a moment. Something that would allow him to be a better version of himself, to help him let go of his anger.

If we as human beings have the desire and power to change in such a deep way then I absolutely believe in hypnosis, suggestion, magic and anything else that offers hope in a world that sometimes feels hopeless.

Take care, Reggie Houser, and remember: "know your own mind".

Michael Gareth.

P.S. If you don't know what I did when I hypnotized you, I am guessing you may still be looking for a true friend? I hope you recognize them soon.

I read the letter over and over, memorizing every word and frowning at the P.S. What does he mean? I found my friends, the hypnosis worked, but it's all just gone horribly wrong. I wish I could talk to him about Saturday. Tell him my plan and ask his advice. I think he would approve. I think what I'm doing is right. I'm making the right choice for a change. I just wish it wasn't so risky.

DO TRY THIS AT HOME!

THE ARM SINK

Don't worry, I am not going to make you wash your arms in the sink. For this one, you need another human volunteer. Ask them to lie down on the floor on their belly and put their arms above their head. (When they have done this feel free to add in the joke of sneaking out of the room and seeing how long they stay there for.) Lift their arms up and hold them in the air for a minute. Then slowly lower them down back towards the floor. They will start freaking out when it feels like their arms are literally going through the floor.

CHAPTER TWENTY-TWO

DO NOT listen in when people are talking about you, however tempting it may be. It never ends well. Remember the time you listened to the popular gang at primary, and Sol Bridger called you a turd.

By the time Saturday comes, I'm a nervous wreck. I've barely slept a wink all week. My body is in a constant fidget. I've been told off in almost every single lesson for calling out, talking, tapping, wriggling, being late, dropping things and forgetting things.

My attempts at self-hypnosis have been dismal. Every time I sit down my eye starts twitching as if it knows that I'm about to try and shut it and calm my brain down. The energy shoots through my twitching eyelid just to remind me that it will not close, whatever I do.

Mum is fed up. I heard her on FaceTime to Dad last night, talking in a whisper about me.

"I saw his light on at three a.m. last night. He's all over the place," she said.

"He's just a kid. That's what kids do," Dad said. "It'll all be OK, love." But even he didn't sound convinced.

"He's doing this dog thing tomorrow and you know what he's like. It will end up being a total catastrophe."

I felt sick when I heard her say that. What if it is a catastrophe like everything else that I ever try and do? What if it goes wrong? Badly wrong and I end up getting into the kind of trouble you see on telly with sirens and handcuffs. Maybe I should just tell her and let the grown-ups deal with it after all. But if Blane finds out I've told on them I honestly think he would kill me. I've got to at least try the plan. There is a chance it could work, and Lily keeps telling me that I can do it.

I've been popping over to Barnaby's after school and I think he's ready. When I showed him an umbrella he went completely ballistic so I think that part of the plan should work just fine. The only problem will be if the dogs don't work as a pack. If any of them have their own ideas.

I'm meeting the gang at three on the high street. I told them all to bring an umbrella, to be ready to be hypnotized, and to wear something pink and something spotty.

The spotty thing I said at the last minute because I wanted to make them look silly, and it made me laugh to think that they trusted me so much that they truly think wearing something pink and spotty will help them to rob a bank. But also making them commit and say yes to things will just heighten their senses. It will hopefully make them more ready to be hypnotized.

I'm calling for the dogs and gathering them all up on their leads. Knocking on doors and smiling at their owners, trying to focus on what they're telling me.

"Tinks loves ear strokes but hates aeroplanes."

"Bonnie will steal anything. Once she ate a plastic bag, so watch her."

"Sapphire vomits when she is nervous."

"Rufus is a darling, but he will chase smart cars. Not sure why but he hates them."

I nod and try to listen to all of the instructions and problems that people have with their beloved pooches. I say the same thing to them all.

"We will have a great time. You just enjoy the fireworks and I'll bring them back afterwards." I'm hoping this is true. Maybe not the part about having a great time, but definitely the part about bringing them back afterwards.

With five dogs pulling in five directions, it's hard to walk towards the high street. I stop at the park and turn to the doggy gang. I look at Barnaby and he immediately sits. It's like I have complete control over him without even saying anything. I smile. My star student. Then the dog next to him sits, and slowly but surely all of the dogs start to sit in a chain reaction. This is what I'm counting on, herd mentality. As they all look up at me with their various funny little faces, waiting for instruction, I feel really positive. I touch each dog gently on their snout and when they close their eyes I know I can do it. I click my fingers and they open their eyes and stand to attention.

"You can totally do this, guys," I say. "Now walk slowly and calmly and follow me, please."

As we all set off, not one of them pulls on the lead. They are a team, and I am their leader. I send calm energy down through the leads and I can feel the power of their energy coming back up and filling me with the confidence I need for the day.

I see Lily waving wildly from our meeting spot. As I approach, there is something different about her. It takes me a moment to register but then my eyes widen.

"Your hair!" I gasp. "It's all gone!"

"I know!" She grins, stroking her short, simple haircut. "I love it!"

"But why? What about your sister?"

"I just thought if you can do this, then surely I can tell my sister I don't want to be a glittery, sparkly Barbie doll any more. It's fine, wanting to please people, but not if you are ignoring yourself. Anyway, I let her cut it, so she was pretty chuffed actually." I smile. I feel proud of her but also proud of me. I recognized that she was not being true to herself, maybe I helped her in a tiny way.

She looks at the collection of mutts who are sitting beautifully at my feet, pats the little scruffy one on the head and says, "Right, introduce me to the gang!"

All of the dogs love Lily and I have to work very hard to get them to stop licking her and come back and sit at my feet. When I have them there, I tap their furry foreheads and get them into a doggy trance. Then I go through the plan, telling them everything that I need them to do. I show them the treats that I have for each of them. When I agreed to calm the dogs for the fireworks, I told the owners that I would need treats. I hold out their favourite things and they sit and drool and somehow make their eyes even bigger. Cheese for Tinks, a sausage for Rufus, chicken for Sapphire, some ham for Bonnie and an apple for Barnaby.

"An apple? What kind of dog likes apples?" asks Lily when she sees it.

"Barnaby. They're his favourite things," I say. Then I pass over the treats to Lily and make sure that the pack have all seen her put them into her bag.

"That apple is what is going to get these dogs to listen to you. That apple is the most important thing you have, Lily." I have not told Lily that my biggest worry with the plan is her. She has to get the dogs under control, and without me there to hypnotize them. I have no idea if she will manage it.

I turn to the dogs and to Lily and talk in a low, calm voice telling them that they are a pack and that Lily is the pack leader. I tell her how she is going to feel in control at all times and I tell the dogs that when she calls them they will listen, and if they listen they will get their treats. They are all quiet and still and tilting their heads this way and that, seemingly taking in everything I have said. I look at my watch.

"It's time for me to go," I say. "You know where you need to be and what you need to do?"

"Yes," Lily says confidently, taking the leads. The dogs immediately start licking her all over and I'm not sure if she will be able to get them anywhere, let alone to the high street at the exact time she needs to be there.

"I don't have a back-up plan, Lily, so you need to be there at four o'clock exactly, OK?"

"Yup! Got it," she calls from underneath a pile of fur and tongues. "Don't worry, Reggie."

I turn to go and can't help but worry. What if this all goes horribly wrong? I don't want to end up in a prison cell or, if Blane gets hold of me, a hospital.

When I get to the side street where the gang agreed to meet, it's completely empty. My heart leaps for a second when I think that maybe they have had second thoughts. But then I see them and have to stop myself snorting with laughter. They look ridiculous. They have cut-out pink spots attached to their hoodies and combats, stuck on with glue that still looks wet. Each of them is carrying a different umbrella. I nearly howl when I see Blane carrying a small Peppa Pig one with frills. They look a whole mix up of things – embarrassed, scared and wild-eyed, but mainly ridiculous.

"I don't know why we had to wear this stupid stuff," I hear Vince saying, and I take a breath in and take control.

"You look perfect. The spots will trigger a response in Bob. You are all part of the hypnotic process." They immediately calm down and listen as though I'm some sort of genius. I can't believe they are falling for this nonsense. As if glued-on pink spots could make someone hypnotized, but I carry on.

"You need to be visible to Bob on his way into the bank. Do not make eye contact. Now the next part is very important. On his way out of the bank, Bob cannot see you or the spots. If he sees you, it will not work. That's when you have to put the umbrellas up. Stand behind them and don't even think about peeking. If you peek, everything will go wrong, and we could all end up in prison for a very long time, OK?"

They all nod seriously. One of Oscar's spots slowly peels from his trousers and silently lands on the pavement.

"Now I need to hypnotize you," I say.

"Why?" says Max.

"If you get caught you need to stay calm. You need to stick to the same story. If you are hypnotized, you will be able to do that. If you don't want me to hypnotize you then you are on your own."

"Just let him do it, Max," says Blane, a tremor of fear in his voice that I've never heard before.

A wave of fear washes over me as I start to hypnotize them. What if I can't do it? I'm so much better than I was when I tried before. I'm pretty sure I can get them all to go under. Especially as they are all in a heightened state and they will really want it to work this time. Hypnotism works best when people believe in it and they all really believe in it now. I do a quick induction and when they all have their eyes closed and seem to be in a deep state of hypnosis I begin in my low, slow voice.

"You will show your spots to Bob. At three fifty-five you will put your umbrellas up in front of you to block the spots. You will not peek, however tempted you are. You will definitely not peek." I hear my voice sounding calm and clear, and carry on. "If anything goes wrong, you will run, keeping the umbrellas up, and you will run to the park. There is a bandstand there where we will meet." Then I add the most important bit. The bit that I hope they will hold on to. I look at their flickering eyelids and see Oscar peeking out from under his. He looks scared. He's not hypnotized, and I know it, but there's nothing I can do. I have to keep going.

"If the plan does not work and we meet at the bandstand, you will give up on hypnosis. You will never want to try this again or any plan involving me. You will leave me alone at school, you may even be a little scared of me. You will think twice about doing anything like this ever again and whenever you are tempted to do something bad, you will shudder and remember the sound of barking."

I look and see Oscar's forehead scrunch up in confusion so I carry on quickly.

"When I count to three, you will open your eyes and do everything I have told you. One, two, three."

Their eyes open and I look at my watch and then out on to the high street. 3.45. The security van will be here any minute.

All of a sudden, I lose my calm. I don't know if I can do this. My whole body starts shaking and my brain is so fuzzy that I can barely think. Maybe it would be easier to go along with Blane's plan. If this goes wrong, I have no doubt they will hurt me. I remember the hand around my neck and the look on Blane's face as he held Lily down. He is willing to rob a bank so he wouldn't think twice about beating me to a pulp if I mess it all up.

DO TRY THIS AT HOME!

THE CHAIR LIFT

So hopefully by now you will have gained a lot of friends/worshippers/ followers by using all of your amazing mind skills. You need four of them for this one. Put a chair in the middle of the room and ask one of them to sit in it. The four of you that are left clasp your fingers and point your index fingers out like a gun. Now with two people's fingers under the armpits and two under the knees you all try to lift the seated person. Any lift? Probably not. Now all of you place alternating hands above your friend's head. At this point you can say something about "energy fields" and "the power of the group" when the hands have been there for a while place them back under the person, count down from

3-O and try the lift again. This time
you should be able to lift the person
much more easily. How does it work,
I hear you cry? No one really knows.
Maybe it really is magic!

CHAPTER TWENTY-THREE

WEAR YOUR WATCH!

When you need to be somewhere on time,
you need your watch or you'll get distracted
and will definitely be late. Like the time
you said you would meet Mum at the shops
after school and you got sidetracked by your
shoelaces and turned up an hour late.

When the van pulls up, I rub my face with my hands,
trying to get rid of the doubts in my mind. I can't
see any sign of Lily and the dogs, which is good, I
suppose. I don't want the gang seeing them, otherwise
they will figure it all out. I've moved away from the
others, leaving them to show their spotty bodies to

Bob, who gets out of his van and whistles as he takes out what must be the empty cases from the van.

As he heads to the bank, I move towards the back of the van. The spot where I'm supposed to be hypnotizing him into giving me a case full of cash. I'm hoping and praying that Lily is where she needs to be. My heart is beating fast, but I keep control of my breath and stay as calm as I can. I tell myself that there is no need to be scared as I'm not actually robbing a bank. I'm not actually doing anything, apart from making some naughty kids dress like fools and get scared silly. It feels a little bit scarier than that though, looking at the bank and the van and knowing what I am supposed to be doing. What the gang think I'm about to do.

As I wait for him to emerge, I wonder if I could actually do it. Would it be possible to hypnotize Bob and just tell him that one of the cases belongs to me? Would he hand over thousands of pounds and watch me as I walk away with it? Would it even be classed as stealing if he gave it to me? My brain drifts off and starts thinking about what I would spend the money on. Maybe a go-kart or my own swimming pool. Maybe I could get me and Mum a bigger house with a huge garden for Dad to potter about in. Then I hear a sound of snuffling and snorting coming from the other side of the van and I know that Lily has made it.

I hear a little sneeze. I smile and silently thank Lily for getting here at the perfect moment and for bringing me back out of my daydream. I don't want to steal anything, even if it would get me a pool and a go-kart and a whole load of friends.

I check my watch. 3.59. I look over to the gang and give them the nod. I know that at least one of them will peek even though I hypnotized them and told them not to. That's why Lily has to stay hidden. It has to look like the dogs have come from the van. Also, Barnaby can't see the umbrellas until Bob is back here. I need the gang to think that I tried. That I was attempting to hypnotize him when the dogs escaped.

I look at the bank and see Bob emerging with the cases. Over the road the umbrellas are up. They look very strange all in a wall, Peppa Pig in the middle. It's not even raining. Barnaby is sure to notice them immediately.

As Bob approaches, I stand at the back of the van, hoping I don't look too suspicious. Even standing by a security van full of cash makes me feel nervous, like someone might handcuff me for even being here.

Bob nods at me and smiles; he doesn't seem

worried by my presence. I smile back and ask him what the time is. I make sure I do it quietly enough so that the gang can't hear me and will think, if they are peeking, that I'm hypnotizing him.

"About four o'clock, kid," Bob says as he opens the back doors of the van. I nod and thank him, and know that we have to do it now. I turn to the front of the van and see Lily with the dogs, struggling to get the leads off, unable to release the dogs as they pull on their collars. As Barnaby catches sight of the umbrellas, it all happens.

He lurches forward, pulling Lily clean off her feet and the other dogs all follow Barnaby. For a second Lily is dragged along the pavement, arms stretched out ahead and body being pulled in a straight line behind the pack.

"Let go!" I whisper. "Just let go of the leads!"

Eventually she lets go, and I hope that none of the gang have seen the chaos.

The dogs, now free, charge towards the umbrella wall, narrowly avoiding a jogger who spins around to follow the action. Barnaby leads the pack on towards Peppa Pig and from a side road comes a pushchair with a toddler babbling away, happily unaware, until the mother pushing the pram squeals at the oncoming doggy gang. Barnaby sees the buggy just in time and leaps high into the sky over the child's head. The child points his chubby little finger and shouts, "Doggy!" I cover my eyes not wanting to watch, but through a gap in my fingers I see the other dogs one by one leaping and just about clearing the delighted child. With each gargantuan leap the squeal of "Doggy!" can be heard above the traffic.

The next squeal sounds less delighted and comes from behind the umbrella wall. The screams of the gang as they look from behind their shields and realize the dogs are heading their way are loud and clear. I think I hear Blane scream, "Run." And the umbrellas head down the side street and towards the park just like I told them to, with the dogs in hot pursuit.

When they are out of sight, I quickly help Lily up from the floor. She has rips in her leggings and there is blood on her knees.

"Are you OK?" Bob says.

"Yes, I am fine," says Lily. Then she grins at me. "We did it, Reggie! Now you'd better go and get the dogs back." She gives me the bag of treats and I smile at her and then turn and run towards the park. I quickly turn back to check she is OK. Despite the bloody knees, she grins at me with her short hair and puts both thumbs in the air.

We did it, we actually did it! Now I just have to hope the gang do everything I asked them to do. And there is the small issue of getting the dogs back inside before the fireworks all go off. I run towards the park faster than I've ever run before, feeling the wind on my face and sticking my arms out as though I'm flying.

DO TRY THIS AT HOME!

MEMORY LIKE AN ELEPHANT

Strap in, this is a long one! But it's so good that it's worth it.

For this one you need a very big book — like a bible or a dictionary — and a calculator. Firstly you need to memorize the ninth word on page 108. (Don't include titles, use the main body of the text — if it's not obvious which the ninth word is then choose another book.)

Now tell them that you have memorized the entire book. Build this into an elaborate but believable tale. Give them the calculator and ask them to put a three-digit number in it. (Tell them that to make it really difficult make every number different — this is really important as it doesn't work otherwise. So not 223 or 414.) Tell them to reverse the number so if they chose 456 reversed it would be 654. Then tell them to use the calculator and take the smallest number from the largest.

654 − 456= 198

Now ask them to reverse the answer.

198 turns into 891.

Now add them together.

891 + 198 = 1089

The answer will ALWAYS be 1089 if you have explained it correctly and not been distracted by a satsuma or something.

Now ask them to tell you what the first three numbers are. You can then let them or someone else turn to page 108 of the big book. Ask them what the fourth number is and when they say 9 you can ask them to read but not tell you what the ninth word on page 108 is. You will then tell them what the word is, by pretending to go through your enormous memory and selecting the correct word from the correct page of your immense brain. Obviously you can only do this once, or they will quickly discover it's the same number every time. Unless you actually want to memorize a massive book and be truly impressive. I can't really be bothered so will stick with the trick.

CHAPTER TWENTY-FOUR

MOST IMPORTANT THING
TO REMEMBER EVER...

You will be OK.

**Even when you feel like you won't, which
is quite a lot, you will be. You have got
through loads and you will get through loads
more and no matter what, you will be OK.**

As I run towards the bandstand, I see the gang
standing on the small stage surrounded by the dogs.
Barnaby is barking wildly and the others are jumping
up at the little railing around the gang.

With their homemade pink spots and umbrellas
still in the air just like I asked, it looks like the

strangest performance. When I get close enough, I whistle to Barnaby and secretly let the apple drop to the floor. He immediately snuffles it up and looks up to me for more. I need to keep up the act and make the gang think that the dogs are security guards and not just random mutts from my street.

I call to the terrified gang, "Umbrellas down." They do it immediately and then I tell Barnaby to sit. He does and the other dogs all copy him. I see Oscar and Vince watching in amazement.

"How does he do that?" I hear one of them say. I do some phoney moves with my arms as though I am hypnotizing the dogs, and quietly whisper to Barnaby to lie down. When he does, there are gasps from the bandstand.

"Wait," I say to the dogs, and they all lie and watch as I head over to the bandstand, leaving the bag of treats next to them so that they don't follow me.

"You saved our lives," Oscar says.

"That big one was trying to kill us," Vince adds.

Now is my chance to end this whole thing. I look at them and say, "No one told me that Bob had a van full of dogs."

"We didn't know," says Vince. "Honest."

"Well, thanks to you lot, it's ruined. Luckily I

hypnotized Bob into thinking that the dogs had just run off for no reason. He has no idea I was trying to steal one of the cases. Now I need to get the dogs back to him before the hypnosis wears off."

"Thanks, Reggie," says Vince.

"Sorry," mumbles Blane, who is unusually quiet for once.

"I am never doing anything like this again. You can all just leave me alone now, or I will find the dogs and set them on you, OK?"

They all nod and as I turn and gather up the leads, I see Oscar looking at me, eyes slightly narrowed, trying to figure out what on earth has just happened. He looks as if he might speak, then gives a shake of his head and decides against it.

When I get to the park gates I feel a tap on my shoulder and turn to see Oscar, who has left the others and gestures for us to go around the corner out of sight.

"I know the dogs weren't in the van. I saw them."

I pause, waiting to see what he will say next.

"I wasn't hypnotized, I was just going along with it."

"I know," I say. "I could tell." Then I look at him. "Have you told the others?"

"No," he says, then he lowers his voice and whispers, "I'm not going to tell them, not ever."

"Why not?"

"I don't want to go to prison," he says quietly. "I didn't want to do any of that stuff, I was just going along with Blane. We all just do everything he says, but maybe now he will be different. I just wanted to say thank you."

"That's OK," I say and he turns and walks away quickly. I feel sorry for him and for Max and Vince too. For all the kids at school who are going along with things, doing things they don't really want to do just to fit in or because they are scared.

As I leave the park, I turn back one last time and see them all miserably peeling their spots off. A part of me feels sad for them. I wish I could have done more to help them. I wish I could hypnotize them into being better people, making better choices because they want to, not because they are scared of the sound of dogs or because they are scared of me or of getting caught. I guess you can only really hypnotize someone into doing something that deep down they really want to do anyway. Maybe all those kids at school that I turned into chickens or pigs secretly wanted the freedom to cluck or snort. To break out from behaving like everyone else for a few moments. To do something different for a change.

It feels sad walking away from the gang. They were *my* gang, not for very long but bits of it felt great. Being part of something and being protected. Having a role and feeling needed. Having people want to be around me. I know they weren't the right people, but it still felt pretty good.

As I walk back towards the high street, the dogs all walking perfectly by my side, I look around and on one side see people queuing to get on a bus as it opens its doors at the white painted STOP on the tarmac. On the side of the bus is a huge advert of a lady with a shiny face telling me to buy some perfume. On my right I see a couple of little kids running ahead of their parents, one of them roaring and skipping like a tiny little dinosaur, the other laughing and running alongside.

When the tiny T-rex turns to his friend and says, "Roar!" his little friend giggles and roars back. "Louder!" shouts the T-rex and, as requested, the little boy roars again and this time becomes the dinosaur he wants to be.

Maybe we are all hypnotized all of the time. Whether it's stopping at a sign that tells us to stop, making a queue without even being told to do it, buying something that we are told we need or roaring to make our friend feel happy. Are our minds being manipulated into buying the things we buy, looking the way we look or even smelling the way we smell?

Maybe my dreams of being part of a gang were because I had been told so many times that you have to have a group of mates and that they should look and sound and behave in a certain way. Maybe I had been brainwashed into not noticing when a true friend with a heart on her head was sitting right next to me.

I guess sometimes going along with suggestions or making an orderly queue is a good thing, it creates calm and stability, but sometimes we need to question what we are being told. We need to look at ourselves and what we really truly want rather than what we are being told we want or need. We need to know our own minds.

When I get back to the bank, I see Lily waving at me from a bench across the road, her knees still bleeding but a huge smile on her face when she sees the dogs.

"You did it, didn't you?" she says.

"Yeah, I guess I did. We did," I say, feeling proud in a way that I have never felt before. I look at her and smile a grateful smile. "Thanks for being my friend, even when I was horrible to you. Thanks for hanging out with me and being so kind."

As I say the words out loud, it's like I'm waking up from a dream. I look at her face and blink my eyes, not believing what I'm seeing. Her eyes, her face, her hair, it is all so familiar. All of a sudden, I know her. It's like I'm seeing her for the first time.

"Frizz," I whisper. "You're Frizz!"

"Hi, Reggie." She smiles and clicks her fingers. "And he's awake… Finally!"

She giggles at the look of confusion on my face.

"You're Lily but you're Frizz. Have you always been Frizz? Why didn't I recognize you? I've known you forever." I feel a bit scared, as though maybe there is something really wrong with my brain. What has happened to me? Why did I not know her? She can tell that I'm starting to panic.

"I don't understand what's happening to me."

"It was the hypnotist guy."

"Michael Gareth?"

Lily nods and smiles. "Your mum and him thought you weren't seeing me as a true friend. He thought maybe seeing me through fresh eyes might be a good idea."

"But why did you go along with it?" I ask between memories and flashbacks. "I've been horrible to you."

"Well, you were never THAT nice to me anyway, were you? I thought it was really cool, the idea that you could get to know me all over again. Your mum said that if I just kept being me, you would realize what a good friend I was . . . and here we are!"

"I can't believe you kept it a secret."

I can almost hear Michael Gareth's words sounding out clearly somewhere in the depths of my memory.

"When you wake up, you will have no memory of Frizz, the only person who has been consistently kind to you. The person you have ignored. When you see her, you will have no idea who she is. You will forget that her real name is Lily. When she is kind to you, it will help you to see what true friendship can be, but you will only recognize her again when you are ready to be the kind of friend that she deserves."

The words whoosh around my head, and I go back over the last few weeks, remembering the first day of school and her huge grin. Remembering how horrible I was in the dinner hall and her sad, scrunched-up face. Her words coming back to me: "I knew it was a bad idea."

267

"I'm sorry it took me so long," I say, still not fully believing what has happened. "I knew Michael Gareth was good but this is ridiculous!"

"I nearly told you so many times!" She laughs.

"How did you know?" I ask. "You weren't even at Trontin's."

"Your mum told me when we went for a picnic. She thought it was worth a try, so I went along with it. I thought it would be fun."

An image of Michael Gareth and Mum chatting as I went to get cake pops into my brain.

"If all of this was planned, how did he know that I would even make friends with you? I didn't even know you were going to Redwood."

She stops smiling for the first time and looks sad.

"I changed my mind about which school to go to," she says quietly. "The kids in my class at primary were a bit mean so I wanted a fresh start."

"What were they doing?" I ask, realizing that I had never really spoken to Frizz about her life before. I was always so wrapped up in my own stuff at primary school I never knew that she was struggling too.

"I'm different. Kids don't like it, do they? They said I was annoying. Then they all just ignored me. They wouldn't look at me or answer me when I asked them something. They pretended I didn't exist."

"That's horrible," I say, suddenly feeling so sad for my new friend. Sad and angry and guilty, knowing what it feels like to be lonely. Knowing that I treated her exactly the same.

"I only decided at the start of the holidays to change schools and my mum had just told your mum before you went to Trontin's."

"But why did you go along with it? I was the only person you knew. I could have looked after you."

"Would you have though? Anyway, your mum was worried about you, Reggie, and I wanted to help. I thought it would be kind of fun. I so nearly told you in the lunch hall, though."

I drop my head, remembering what I had said about her at Trontin's. That she didn't count.

"I was just as bad as those other kids," I say sadly. "I'm sorry." Then I feel another wave of confusion.

"How did Michael Gareth know it would all work out though, and I wouldn't just carry on ignoring you?"

"I guess he believed in you, like I did and like your mum did. He knew that deep down you wanted a true friend, and you would eventually figure it out and stop trying to hang around with a bunch of losers."

"How did you believe in me? I never did anything to make you believe in me."

"I knew from when we were little and I would come over. I made you play with teddies and you used to tap and hum and wriggle and jiggle. I was poorly and about half the size of other kids my age. I knew that we were both just a bit different. You seemed lost. Like me."

I smile and nod, feeling disorientated.

"Remember, I used to set up a teddy bears' picnic? Have them all sitting round drinking imaginary tea and singing lullabys to them, then you would pretend they were having a food fight and end up throwing them all around the room? It was funny. I like the way your brain works."

"No one likes the way my brain works!"

"Well, I do."

"I'm sorry I was so mean to you, Lily... I mean, Frizz. Lily or Frizz. What do I even call you now?!"

"How about we start over again? Come up with a new name? I never liked being Frizz anyway, that's what my sister called me."

"What about a mixture of Frizz and Lily?"

"FRILLY!" we both shout at the exact same time.

As I'm giggling at her new ridiculous name, which is

270

somehow completely perfect for her, I realize that I don't want this day to end yet. I want to stretch it out forever.

"Do you want to come and watch some fireworks?" I ask.

"What about the dogs?"

"I'll bring them. They love fireworks, or they will do when I've finished with them." Then I turn to my new furry gang, tap each one on the forehead and click my fingers.

As the night lights up above us and the dogs lie snoozing on the grass I feel like everything is going to be OK. When Sapphire's owner sees us, she comes running over, thinking there must be a problem.

"I thought you were keeping them inside. Is she all right?" she says, looking in alarm at Sapphire as she snores through another rocket shooting into the sky.

"She's fine," I say. "We are all enjoying the fireworks. She just needed to know she could relax, that's all."

"I don't know what to say."

"Don't say anything, just enjoy your evening and I'll drop them all back afterwards."

She is about to leave, then hesitates and turns back. "Sapphire is terrified of beards. She goes wild every time she sees one. My brother has a beard; could you do something? He hasn't visited us for years." She looks so sad and hopeful that I can't say no. Then she adds, "I would pay you, obviously."

I smile and nod. Maybe hypnotizing animals is OK. I can't get into trouble doing that, can I?

"I'll come and see her after school on Monday."

Then when I think she is finally going to go back to the fireworks she turns back again.

"Next door have a parakeet who screams at the TV."

"I have never tried to hypnotize a bird, but I can give it a go," I say, wondering how much money I can make from this new business.

I smile as she walks off, looking back at Sapphire, whose feet are now twitching.

"What do you think she's dreaming about?" Frilly asks.

"Normally I would say chasing rabbits but maybe tonight she's dreaming about chasing umbrellas."

"Do you think they'll leave you alone at school?"

"I think so. They were pretty freaked out by the whole thing."

A huge shower of blue lights explode into the sky, crackling as they fall.

"And what about your hypnosis, will you keep doing it?"

"I don't know. I'll definitely keep doing it on myself and the various pets of the street, but I don't want to get into any more trouble."

"I guess it depends how you use it."

I nod and lie down next to the dogs, softly stroking Barnaby's chest and watching the sky light up. I think I need to find friends like Frilly, who like me for me, not because I can hypnotize people.

As we lie there listening to the sizzles and bangs, I hear a familiar voice.

"Look at you two!"

I sit up and see Mum and Dad standing arm in arm and smiling down at us.

"Dad! You're back!" I say as I jump to my feet.

"Hello, son. I popped back for the weekend."

As I hug him tightly I see Mum's face as she smiles and winks at Frilly.

"Yes, Mother," I say loudly. "I figured out your and Michael Gareth's little plan. I thought 'hypnosis was dangerous'!"

"Well, you didn't deserve Frizz, the way you were behaving, so I thought it was worth a chance... Anyway, it looks like it worked." She looks at Frilly.

"Don't let him be mean to you, Frizz, OK? You need to stand up to him."

"Don't worry, I will," she says.

Dad gestures for me to walk with him and as we take a few steps away from the sleeping dogs, I can hear Frilly explaining her new name to Mum and re-enacting the moment that I recognized her.

"You OK, Dad?" I ask.

"Yes, son, I'm fine. I was thinking about what you said last weekend. About me being like you, with the ADHD."

"Well, I didn't say that, Dad, I just wondered."

"I think you might be right, son, that's all." I look at him and I can see that this is hard for him to say. That the words are not easy.

"I just wanted to say sorry," he says.

"What for?"

"For not figuring it out. Maybe if I had known I could have been a bit more use to you, shown you a better way. Helped you." I look at his tired face and I feel so sad for him that he has never had anyone understand him. I feel sad that he feels bad for me when actually he should feel bad for himself. After all, I have Frilly, I have Mum, I have hypnosis and I have all the dogs in the world and now I even have him. I feel happier and luckier than I have ever felt before.

"You're helping me now, Dad," I say, smiling.

"I don't know about that," he says.

"You are. Just being here and saying that. It makes me feel less alone. Thanks, Dad. I love you." I think about how Frilly made me feel better about myself by liking my brain. I wonder if Dad needs someone like that too. Maybe I can be that person for him. The person who likes him exactly the way he is. So I tell him.

"I like the fact you never finish a project or never sit down for more than a minute. I like that we both get up in the night and can't sleep. I like that your brain is different like mine. I think you are great, Dad, different, but great."

"Ruddy Nora, I didn't come back here to cry like a baby," he says as he wipes his eyes.

"Maybe now we can help each other a bit," I say.

"You're not ruddy hypnotizing me, that's for sure," he says, laughing, but he pulls me in tightly for a hug and I feel a prickle in my eyes as we squeeze each other tightly.

When the fireworks are over I can feel my brain fizzing. As though it's not ready to switch off yet.

Images of the day and night are buzzing around, overlapping with each other. The colours and sounds of barking, umbrellas and fireworks. I try to breathe and imagine walking down some steps to calm it down and then I look around me at the emptying field and down the hill next to us and know exactly what I want to do.

"Frilly, this may be a weird question…"

"Go on, I love a weird question."

"Do you want to roll down the hill with me?"

DO TRY THIS AT HOME

A DINNER-TIME TRICK

When you are sitting down to tea, maybe you all have a lovely pudding in front of you. Ask everyone at the table to close their eyes and picture a playing card — any card. They will groan, roll their eyes and do what you say. Now eat as much of their tasty puddings as you can before they catch on, open their eyes and send you to your room for being annoying.

ACKNOWLEDGEMENTS

Thanks to all of the usual suspects. My agents and publishers and all of the fabulous humans who made this book happen.

I would like to thank Rupert and his mum for having me over to chat. It was lovely and you are brilliant!

Thanks to Imogen and Mum for reading an early draft and to Cleo for listening to me read it again and again. So helpful.

Thanks to all of my friends and family who have allowed me to try and hypnotize them for the last year. You will all be glad to know it's over now and I won't try and turn you into chickens ever again.

Thanks to Rob, Eva and Lenny for coming up with the best insults.

Massive thanks to all the bookshops, librarians and teachers who share all the bookish love. You are wonders.

Biggest thanks to all the kids who read my books… if you are still reading to this point then I am very impressed, you are clearly the best of all the kids, so well done you!

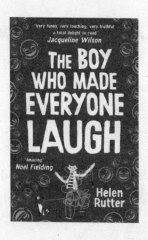

Billy is an eleven-year-old boy with a big dream. He wants to be a stand-up comedian when he grows up: delivering pinpoint punch-lines and having audiences hang on his every hilarious word. A tough career for anyone, but surely impossible for Billy, who has a stammer. How will he find his voice, if his voice won't let him speak?

"This incredible debut tugs at your heartstrings and makes you laugh out loud in equal measure. I guarantee you'll be cheering along in the final pages!"
Lisa Thompson, bestselling author of *The Goldfish Boy*

"It's *Wonder* with one-liners."
Scott Evans, The Reader Teacher

WINNER OF THE LAUGH-OUT-LOUD BOOK AWARDS 2023
SHORTLISTED FOR THE BLUE PETER BOOK AWARD 2022
SHORTLISTED FOR THE COSTA CHILDREN'S BOOK AWARD 2022

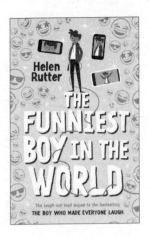

Billy Plimpton is on the road to stand-up comedy stardom – and he won't let his stammer hold him back! Until everything goes wrong at his first gig and Billy decides to stop telling jokes forever. But when celebrity comedian Leo Leggett posts a social media clip of Billy, he suddenly becomes the most famous funny kid in the country. It's everything Billy has ever dreamed of!

Or is it? Billy can't shake the feeling that the world of showbusiness might not be as shiny as it seems. Will he keep his feet on the ground, remember who his real friends are, and realize that being true to himself is what makes him a star?

"Fun, unstuffy and wise"
Sunday Times Children's Book of the Week

"A delight...
This book is wise,
suspenseful and witty"
Sunday Times Children's
Book of the Week

Archie Crumb is having a tough time. Picked-on at school, picked last for any team; his home has been sad and quiet since Dad left and his luck feels like its run out. But things start looking up when Archie bumps his head and literally sees stars: his favourite famous football player standing in front of him, granting him nine wishes. This is INCREDIBLE! Unlimited ice cream, a whole day of eating pizza and playing on the X-Box, revenge on the bullies, becoming the star player in a televised football tournament: finally, all his dreams can come true! Will Archie wish his way to happiness? Or will he realise that magic wishes may be wonderful, but only he has the true power to change his life?

TURN OVER TO READ THE FIRST CHAPTER!

CHAPTER ONE

**You always have to believe in your dreams.
—Lucas Bailey, star striker of Valley Rovers**

**I dreamed last night that I was being eaten
by a giant hamster. —Archie Crumb**

My mum used to tell me to make wishes all the time.
At all the usual things – blowing out candles on a
cake, catching a dandelion clock in the air, spotting
a rainbow – but there were a million other reasons
to wish too.

If we said something at the exact same time:

"Make a wish!"

If we ever saw a feather, or a bird of any kind –
even a scabby, one-legged pigeon:

"Make a wish, Archie!"

Even the most disgusting things:

"Ergh, Mum, there's one of your hairs in my fried egg!"

"Make a wish, Archie. Quick!"

"Erm ... I wish there wasn't a hair in my fried egg?!"

If we walked under a bridge when a train went by, if I bumped my elbow, if wind blew leaves into my face or if snow started falling. Every single thing was worth a wish, according to my mum.

"If you don't wish for it, then it can't come true, can it?"

When you have to make so many wishes, it's hard to know what to wish for. I went through all of the usual things: becoming a millionaire, being able to fly, more wishes, cool trainers. None of those wishes came true – I don't think they ever do. Not mine anyway.

My name is Archie Crumb and I'm a pretty useless person. I'm one of those kids who can't really do anything, and I mean ANYTHING. Most people, if they are not so good at something like maths, are usually pretty good at another thing like art. Those kids who are rubbish at school lessons generally head out into the playground at lunch and can run really fast or jump super high or score every goal in football.

Even Felix Ratton in my class, who is worse than me at spelling, can take a lawnmower apart and put it back together again. We didn't know that till he won a prize at the school fair. The prize was to be the teacher for a day (sounds more like a punishment than a prize, if you ask me!). Everyone thought Felix would be a terrible teacher, but it was the best day ever! He told us he has six lawnmowers at home that he found in skips or by people's bins. He took them home and fixed them. Apparently he's always on the lookout for a broken lawnmower. He can even recognize the make by its sound. None of us knew anything about his love for lawnmowers until the day he became our teacher.

The day after Felix's lesson, when I was at my dad's, I tried to take his brand-new lawnmower apart and put it back together again, to see if that was my hidden talent too. I ended up sweating, surrounded by bits of metal and screws with absolutely no idea where any of them were meant to go. Dad and Julie were furious. Lawnmowers are definitely not my secret gift. I still haven't found out what is, and I'm starting to lose hope.

Teachers always say that everyone is good at something. Not me. I come bottom in EVERYTHING.

I have absolutely no special skills. I'm bad at every lesson, I can't do my times tables, my spelling is hideous, my handwriting looks like spiders and the last time I drew my mum a picture she thought it was a teapot when it was meant to be a ship. Why on earth would I have been drawing a teapot?! I can't run in a straight line without falling over, let alone kick a ball properly. I'm even rubbish at computer games.

Mum doesn't bother telling me to wish any more, not now that she's in bed. Most of the time she's asleep – or pretending to be. I know when she's pretending; it's all down to the breathing. I used to do that too, when I was little. The trick is to breathe super slowly. When I get in from school and put my head round the door, I can see her eyes closed, just above the duvet, but I can see her breath making the covers go up and down, too fast for real sleep.

I'm not sure why she pretends. I think maybe she's too tired to talk. That's OK – I just go and sort out my football stickers and eat spaghetti hoops straight out of the tin.

Sometimes I take my spaghetti and snuggle up in bed too, with my stickers, making lists of who I need to get and who I have already got. I love the red, shiny packets and I know all of the stats and facts about the players. On the back of every packet is where I get all my best inspirational quotes. A bit like the pictures Julie has in the living room that say LIVE LAUGH LOVE – but better. I love these quotes – expecially the Lucas Bailey ones – and I always try to follow their advice, but sometimes it doesn't work out.

How can you follow your dreams if you don't even know what your dreams are? I have no idea what I want to do with my life, and I can't understand how other kids seem to already know – we're only eleven! Everyone seems to have it all worked out: Mouse wants to be a lawyer, Martha wants to be a dog groomer, Kiran wants to be an ice-skater and most of the boys want to be footballers.

There is no chance of me EVER being a footballer and so I'll stick with my stickers – get it? *Stick* with my *stickers*! I have a HUGE pile of doubles, probably the biggest in the school. Some kids do the most stupid swaps, like fifty doubles for one shiny, but I love my doubles pile. I keep all of my Lucases together in a separate pile. I have fifty-two Lucas Baileys. He's my favourite. Last season he scored thirty-five goals and was the top scorer. He's from round here too; he used to go to my school. There are pictures of him all over the corridors and a massive display in reception with newspaper clippings and interviews he's done.

Sometimes I talk to him. I know it sounds stupid and I get a bit scared that talking to a sticker might mean that I'm bonkers – but I do. If stickers had little ears and could hear then he would know so much about me. He would know that Mouse is my best friend and that she's better at football than any of the other girls at school and most of the boys too – if she was given a chance. We practise penalties in her garden, and I have NEVER seen her miss one. She's amazing.

He would know that the B-B Gang are horrible and say mean things about EVERYONE. He would know that I cheated and looked at Martha's maths test today. He would also know that I then felt so bad and so worried, I scribbled all of the answers out and got zero out of twenty.

He would know that nine is my lucky number because it's the number on his shirt, and that sometimes I say things nine times in my head to try and make them happen or tap things on the table nine times to bring me good luck. He would be the only person in the world who knows that Mum has only got out of bed once this week.

She'll get better; she says she just needs time. I know she's trying. She booked us a holiday to Scarborough last Easter and we spent weeks talking about the slot machines and the sea. Then the week before we were meant to go, she started staying in bed again. Longer and longer. Saying how much her head hurt. I knew straight away that the holiday was off. The day before we were meant to get the train she was crying and saying how bad she felt. I ended up having to tell her that it was OK even though it didn't feel OK.

That's sometimes what happens with Mum: she steals all the feelings so there are none left for me. There was the time that I was meant to have a proper birthday party sleepover with popcorn and a movie. We'd tidied up the house and everything. The day I was taking invites into school she went very shaky and said that she was not ready to have a house full of people and so I just went to Mouse's for my birthday tea instead.

There's always a reason why she can't go to every single school play, sports day and parents' evening. It's just the way it is; it's not her fault, is it? She doesn't want to be like this. So why do I sometimes feel so angry with her?

Mum says I'm not allowed to tell anyone that she stays in bed. They'll get all worried and involved and that's the last thing she needs. If she's too tired to chat to *me* some days, then imagine how bad it would be if we had teachers ringing her all the time.

When I go to Dad's, he'll say, "How's your mum?" but I know it's not a real question. There are loads of questions that aren't real. Sometimes I see grown-ups pass each other on the street and say, "Hi. You all right?" without even stopping to hear the answer – that's not a real question, is it, so what's the point in asking it? It's the same with Dad. He doesn't want the real answer and so I always just say, "The same."

That seems to satisfy him. I don't want to lie and that feels like the truth – but not the whole truth. I HATE lying. My dad's a liar. When I was seven, he told me the biggest lie ever. I heard him and Mum shouting in the kitchen and when I went downstairs, he told me not to worry.

"Everything's going to be OK, Archie," he said.

Well, it wasn't. They kept shouting in the kitchen for months, until one day he left. Now he's married to Julie, who has shiny skin and dangly earrings. They had my sister, Scadge, who he clearly loves way more than me. That's when Mum started feeling bad and needing to rest. A year ago she lost her job and so now she has nothing to get out of bed for anyway.

Everything was not "OK". So now I don't really

believe anything he says.

I go to Dad and Julie's house every other weekend. I like going so I can see Scadge, even though she's spoiled rotten and gets anything she wants. She really makes me laugh. She's three. Her name is actually Scarlett, but I call her Scadge. Julie HATES it.

"Archie, please don't call her that. It makes her sound like an urchin."

Scadge loves it though. Whenever Julie tells me off, she sings, "Scadgy Scadgy Scadgy scoo!" and makes farting sounds with her tongue.

"Delightful!" Julie always says, and me and Scadge just burst out laughing and carry on singing the Scadge song.

She's completely obsessed with unicorns; her whole bedroom is covered in them and it always smells like sherbet. Julie puts her in frilly white dresses and only lets her play with one toy at a time.

It's my weekend with Dad now. Today, when I get there, I take Scadge into the perfect back garden, which looks like every blade of grass has been trimmed with hairdressing scissors, and teach her how to kick a football. She's the only person in the world who I can beat at football. She loves it and squeals every time she tries to kick the ball.

Then she gets overexcited and starts squealing and dancing, falls over the ball, gets mud all over her dress, and of course I get into trouble.

"What on earth do you look like, Scarlett Rose! Well, thank you, Archie, thank you very much!" Julie snaps. "Now, go and get changed and find something tidy to do."

Scadge goes up to get changed and fetch a unicorn board game for us to play and Dad goes into the kitchen. Which leaves me and Julie on our own.

I feel big in their house, even though I'm actually pretty small. I end up knocking things over and spilling drinks and then there's a flurry of panic to get it all perfect again. So far I haven't broken anything or bumped into anything this weekend, but there's still time.

I don't think Julie likes my visits much. She always looks really uncomfortable and if we're ever left in a room alone together, she makes this sound like a cross between a laugh and a sigh. She makes that noise now.

"Hah'mmmm."

I'm not sure what the noise means but it makes me feel weird. Am I meant to do the noise back to her? Or say something? Or just sit in the weird silence that follows it?

After a bit of awkward breathing in and out I say the first thing that pops into my head.

"How come your sofa smells so sweet?"

Julie's whole face lights up.

"I use a fifty-fifty mix of fabric conditioner and water, in a little spray bottle. Here!" She takes a pretty glass bottle out of a drawer and asks if I want to "give it a squirt".

I take the bottle. It is shaped like a cloud and is made out of beautiful clear glass with blue swooshes through it. It looks like it should hold expensive perfume, not just sofa spray. I hold it out carefully, and after feeling the shape of the bottle and staring at the pattern in the glass I give it a squirt.

"The fabric conditioner is called Summer Breeze and it is my favourite smell ever," she says. She closes her eyes and breathes in deeply. She looks really happy and relieved now that we have found something to talk about.

As I sit there smelling the Summer Breeze, I wonder how many other eleven-year-old boys Julie has met. I'm guessing not many.

The next time I do a food shop I'm going to look for some Summer Breeze fabric conditioner so that our sofa smells as good as Julie's. It'll probably be too expensive though. I've tried to clean our house and make it sparkle, but it never does. There are stains on the carpet from where I spilled some tomato soup and it always smells a bit disgusting, no matter what I do.

When I'm at home, I can't smell the badness. It's when I go out and come back in again that I notice it. I'm not sure why that happens. Maybe I get used to whatever is rotten and my brain makes it disappear, like magic.

After I've let Scadge beat me three times at her new game, Julie calls us in for lunch. There are matching plates, and the cutlery all has red spotty handles. Scadge is chattering on about how she beat me.

"Next time you come round, Archibald, I will beat you again and again and again!" she says, cackling.

I wish I had never told her that some people called Archie are actually called Archibald. She's not stopped calling me it ever since. Dad laughs too. But then he clears his throat and pulls his serious face, and I know something bad is coming.

"Talking of next time, Archie..." There's a pause as he eats some noodles. "I'm afraid we're going to have to rearrange the weekend after next."

I know what "rearranging" means – it means

cancelling. Dad is constantly "rearranging" our weekends. He doesn't look at me as he slurps up a dangling noodle.

"Julie's friend has offered us their caravan in Wales for the weekend, so we couldn't say no."

Julie makes the weird noise again, "Hah'mmmm," and we all sit there feeling weird. Even Scadge is quiet for once. Our cutlery clinks on our plates.

Then I say in a voice that comes out louder and far less casual than I want, "Can I come too?"

"Yes!" shouts Scadge, dropping her spoon into her bowl.

"I want Archibald to come too! Then I can take my game and beat him again and again and again."

Dad blinks, then he ruffles her hair.

"He can't, sweetie," he says. He's pretending to talk to Scadge, but I know he's really talking to me. "We would all love for him to come but the caravan's really tiny, and he is a big lad now. I'm sure he wouldn't want to be squished in with us for a whole weekend!"

The truth is that I would love to be squished in and, just as I'm about to say so, I knock my fork out of my bowl and send it flying towards the gleaming white tiles. Julie sucks her breath in and starts making little tweeting sounds as she flaps about and cleans it up.

"See, Scarlett, Archie in a caravan would just not work!" Then Dad chuckles and ruffles my hair too, as if everything's sorted.

"So, shall I come next weekend instead?" I ask. Dad darts a glance at Julie.

"Well, it's Scarlett's birthday next weekend..." he says slowly.

"Pleeeease!" begs Scadge.

"Erm..."

"Pleeeeeeeease!"

Dad looks at Julie again, who shrugs and gives a little nod.

"Of course you should come. What a good idea!" Dad says cheerfully, but it feels like he doesn't really think it's such a good idea at all. After a few seconds Julie makes the laugh/sigh sound again.

"Hah'mmmm."

All of a sudden, I feel like I want to get out of this house with its shiny surfaces and sweet smell. I can't wait until four o'clock, when I can ride over to Mouse's for tea.

I don't want to think I'm not welcome at my dad's house. I tell myself that it's all in my head and that they don't mean to make me feel this way. I focus on how much Scadge loves me and how much fun we have. But when I see Dad and Julie look at each other like that – when I see the panic in their eyes at the thought of dealing with me for two weekends in a row – I know that this will never feel like a home for me.

The problem is that my real home doesn't feel like a home either. Proper homes don't smell bad and have someone in bed pretending to sleep all the time, do they? So I'm not sure where that leaves me.